PRAISE FOR

When I Was a Young Man

"Unexpectedly moving... Achieves more grace and dignity than is to be found in the words of most of those who have done time in the U.S. Senate."
— *The Washington Post*

"[An] ineffably sad, tormented, and wonderful book."
— *The New York Review of Books*

"Painful, poignant, and enigmatic."   — *USA Today*

"[Kerrey] tells his story with candor, simplicity and dignity, explaining himself with plain-spoken eloquence and near-mathematical precision."   — *The New York Times*

"Refreshingly honest and often witty." — *Chicago Tribune*

"An astonishing, wonderful book. A distinguished example of that classic American genre, the tale of lost innocence."
— *Time*

"Kerrey is a good writer, an actual writer.... And he's got a great story to tell."   — *Esquire*

"The young men who fought in [the Vietnam War]...
never again were the same. If they survived, they were
changed; the war was their defining experience. Few stories more eloquently testify to such change than that of former U.S. Senator Bob Kerrey." —*Los Angeles Times*

"A remarkable record of a journey to self-knowledge...
Echoes the deceptive simplicity of his fellow Nebraskans,
the novelists Willa Cather and Wright Morris. This sen-
sitive, thoughtful and perceptive book becomes him."
—*Chicago Sun-Times*

"Provides fresh insights into the Vietnam War era as seen
through the eyes of a thoughtful young man whose insu-
lar upbringing in the American heartland had kept him
shielded from moral ambiguity until he confronted it in
the rice paddies of Southeast Asia."—*Houston Chronicle*

"Succeeds on multiple levels: It is a book that manages to
convey the angst of Vietnam without histrionics, it is
emotionally honest and effectively conveys Kerrey's ironic
sense of humor, and it is briskly paced and not overly
maudlin." —*Portland Oregonian*

"Congratulations, Bob Kerrey, for a work so authentic, elo-
quent, haunting, and, finally, uplifting. A classic of its
kind." —*Lincoln Journal Star*

"An extraordinary work of honesty, a coming-of-age story
about a different kind of bravery."
—*The San Diego Union-Tribune*

"Exceptional . . . Soul-searching, brutally frank. "
                    —*Vietnam Veterans of America Magazine*

"Written in short, bluff sentences like the swipes of a scythe through a Nebraska wheat field, [this book is] utterly without posturing, pretense, or braggadocio."
                              —*BusinessWeek.com*

"Bob Kerrey has always been one of the most intriguing of our public figures—independent, winning, yet distant and unpredictable, always slightly out of reach. This memoir, exceptionally well-written, helps explain the man. It is not so much a hero's celebration of his youth as it is the anti-hero's lament for the loss of it."
                              —David Halberstam

"A haunting and ruthlessly honest memoir and a tale of triumph over adversity which provides a lesson for America in a new time of challenge and anxiety."
                    —Haynes Johnson, author of *The Best of Times*

"Bob Kerrey has given so much to his nation. And now more. *When I Was a Young Man* is a narrative of war and loss, yet life enhancing withal."
                              —Daniel Patrick Moynihan

"This story of an American becoming a man is also a story of the country coming of age and it has these classic American virtues: candor, humility, reluctant courage. It is deeply moving and a delight."
                    —Richard Ben Cramer, author of *Joe DiMaggio*

"Bob Kerrey has taken his own life as a hero, shaken it down and out, and produced a memoir of great grace and understanding."

—Jane Kramer, foreign correspondent, *The New Yorker*

"This is an astonishing book, an extraordinary American document, written with a directness and honesty and gravity that offers hope for the country that produced its author."
—Joan Didion

"In this fascinating memoir, Bob Kerrey delivers his version of a traditional American story which beautifully dramatizes his struggle to be honest with himself. This painful exercise of memory results in a work of classic status."

—Paul Fussell, author of *Doing Battle: The Making of a Skeptic, Wartime: Understanding and Behavior in the Second World War,* and *The Great War and Modern Memory*

"An army of readers will embrace this inspiring story."
—*Publishers Weekly* (boxed review)

"An affecting memoir." —*Kirkus Reviews*

"Unlike so many politicians' memoirs, this one is refreshingly honest and a genuinely good story." —*Booklist*

"A deceptively simple yet powerful memoir."
—*Library Journal*

BOB KERREY

When I Was a Young Man

A MEMOIR

A James H. Silberman Book
A HARVEST BOOK • HARCOURT, INC.
Orlando Austin New York San Diego Toronto London

www.HarcourtBooks.com

Library of Congress Cataloging-in-Publication Data
Kerrey, Robert, 1943–
When I was a young man: a memoir/by Bob Kerrey.— 1st ed.
p.   cm.
ISBN 0-15-100474-9
ISBN 0-15-602743-7 (pbk.)
1. Kerrey, Robert, 1943—Childhood and youth.   2. Kerrey, Robert, 1943—
Family.   3. Vietnamese Conflict, 1961–1975—Personal narratives, American.
4. Soldiers—United States—Biography.   5. Lincoln (Neb.)—Biography.
I. Title.
E840.8.K43 A3 2002
959.704'3'092—dc21   2002000764

Text set in Electra
Designed by Linda Lockowitz

Printed in the United States of America

First Harvest edition 2003
K J I H G F E D C B A

AND THE BAND PLAYED
WALTZING MATILDA

Now when I was a young man I carried me pack
And I lived the free life of a rover.
From the Murray's Green Basin to the dusty outback.
Well I waltzed my Matilda all over.
Then in nine-teen fifteen my country said "Son,
It's time you stopped rambling, there's work to be done."
So they gave me a tin hat and they gave me a gun
And they marched me away to the war.

And the band played Waltzing Matilda
As the ship pulled away from the quay.
And 'midst all the cheers the flag waving and tears,
We sailed off for Gallipoli.

And how well I remember that terrible day,
How our blood stained the sand and the water,
And how in that hell that they called Suvla Bay
We were butchered like lambs at the slaughter;
Johny Turk he was ready, he'd primed himself well,
He showered us with bullets and he rained us with shell,
And in five minutes flat he'd blown us all to hell,
Nearly blew us right back to Australia.

And the band played "Waltzing Matilda,"
When we stopped to bury our slain.
We buried ours, and the Turks buried theirs,
Then we started all over again.

And those that were left, well, we tried to survive
In that mad world of blood, death, and fire,
And for ten weary weeks I kept myself alive,
Though around me the corpses piled higher;
Then a big Turkish shell knocked me arse over head,
And when I woke up in my hospital bed,
I saw what I'd done, well wished I was dead,
Never knew there was worse things than dying.

For I'll go no more waltzing Matilda
All around the green bush far and free,
To hump tent and pegs, a man needs both legs,
No more waltzing Matilda for me.

So they gathered the crippled, the wounded and maimed,
And they shipped us back home to Australia,
The legless, the armless, the blind and insane,
Those proud wounded heroes of Suvla;
And when our ship pulled into Circular Quay,
I looked at the place where me legs used to be,
And thanked Christ there was nobody there waiting for me
To grieve, to mourn, and to pity.

But the band played "Waltzing Matilda"
As they carried us down the gangway,
But nobody cheered, they just stood and stared,
Then they turned all their faces away.

And so now every April I sit on me porch,
And I watch the parade pass before me;
I see my old comrades how proudly they march
Reviving old dreams of past glory,
The old men march slowly, old bones stiff and sore,
They're tired old heroes from a forgotten war,
The young people ask: "What are they marching for?"
And I ask myself the same question.

But the band plays "Waltzing Matilda,"
And the old men still answer the call,
But as year follows year, more old men disappear,
Someday no one will march there at all.

To Ben, Lindsey, and Henry

ACKNOWLEDGMENTS

I WOULD LIKE TO THANK Flip Brophy, who was patient when all appeared lost; Barbara Feinman, who nagged me in the beginning; Greg Weiner, who made me feel it was important to write this book; Jim Silberman, who helped me write it well; and my wife, Sarah, who helped me proofread it when I was tired of reading it myself.

PREFACE

THIS IS NOT THE STORY I intended to tell. I wanted this book to be about my father and his brother. That is how it began. After my father's dying request to find out what happened to his only brother, John, during a tour of duty to the Philippines with the United States Army Signal Corps in 1941, I began to examine their past. Their lives began on the other side of the Bolshevik revolution and the First World War, two events that altered their fate and mine.

The story has become more about me than I expected. In part, my plan changed because I never found out enough about John to write the whole story. In part, because I still cannot judge my parents and their generation in an objective way. Mostly, though, the story changed because this is the one I wanted to tell my own children. I wanted to tell it because of the powerful needs that oppose remembering the bad along with the good when we Americans rev up our patriotic engines. The forces of modernity encourage forgetfulness. Terrible stories do not inspire sacrifice the way the noble ones do.

At the 1992 Democratic National Convention in New York City one of our party's leaders—planting a rhetorical flag in the decision by President Harry Truman to confront and contain the expansionist desires of the Soviet Union—repeated a statement I had heard many times since the Soviet Union collapsed in 1991: "We won the Cold War without firing a shot." The audience cheered. Although I knew the speaker meant to say that the United States and the Soviet Union avoided the Third World War that so many had predicted was just around the corner during my lifetime, his words still caused me to wince in pain. We had fired real shots during Korea and Vietnam, and more in Central America, South America, and Africa fighting Cold War battles using proxy soldiers.

As will become clear to anyone who reads this book, I am not a historian. I am a man who has discovered that none of us can isolate ourselves completely from the force of decisions made by men in power. And by living, I am a man who has acquired sympathy—that magic ingredient that turns the bland stew of facts and dates into the rich and flavorful soup of history.

In the first half of my life, history was one of two things: sterile and meaningless information to be memorized for school tests or myths told to generate good feelings and memories. The patriotic and heroic stories I heard in my youth caused me to believe that my nation was never wrong and that my leaders would never lie to me. When the sand of this foundation blew away, I lost my patriotism. In the second half of my life, I rebuilt this foundation on something sturdier: the observation that Americans at their best can be unimaginably generous and willing to put their lives on the line for the freedom and well-being of others.

The story that follows fulfills the promise I made to my father as he lay dying. And it fulfills a promise I made to myself not to forget that wars are not what our slogans, propaganda, and childhood fantasies have taught us to believe.

1

ONE SATURDAY AFTERNOON in the spring of 1954 when I was ten years old, I discovered my father had a brother. My parents, brothers, and sisters were out. I was home alone, a rare and exciting moment, made more exciting by my mission to find a storage room where my mother kept items too important to throw away. My goal was to find a wooden chest that a year earlier I had helped carry into the basement.

I had followed the box's movements from smaller house to larger house during the eight years our family grew from the four small children who arrived in Lincoln, Nebraska, in 1946 following my father's discharge from the U.S. Army, to the seven children who lived there now.

My father's entire name — James Henry Kerrey — was stenciled in black on the top of the faded olive green box. It
had leather handles on either end, a brass-hinged clasp
that held the lid closed, and, fortunately for me, it was not
padlocked.

Our new house was built on three levels. Upstairs
were my parents' master bedroom and two other bedrooms for my sisters. In the basement were four smaller
bedrooms, a large bathroom, and a recreation room for
my brothers and me. In between was the entry level with
spaces used by us all: dining room, music room, living
room, laundry room, and an office.

Under the stairs going to my sisters' and parents'
rooms was a crawl space where the green wooden chest
was stored. That day I carried a chair down to the basement and placed it below the wooden doors that hid my
treasure. As I opened the doors, my heart beat fast from
the fear I might be caught and the excitement of discov-
ering the secrets inside the box. I pulled a string that
switched on a single incandescent bulb and climbed into
the closet, moving things around so I could reach what I
presumed was a war chest full of bloody memorabilia.

As I opened the lid the smell of camphor filled my
lungs. On top were brown wool army jackets, trousers,
and shirts. I pushed the uniforms aside, hoping to find
souvenirs from some great battle. There was nothing of
the sort. No pistols or muddied boots or a jacket with a
bullet hole surrounded by the bloodstain of a fallen com-

rade. No battered helmet marked by too many days on the head of a weary soldier.

Underneath the uniforms I found a bayonet, but the blade looked as new and unused as any hardware knife in my father's store. I found hats, which were too large for my head, and four envelopes of pictures marked Iowa, Florida, Chicago, and Japan. I went straight for the one that said Japan. Inside were three-by-three-inch black-and-white images like the ones we took on our summer vacations. Men in uniforms stood in front of a metal building with a rounded roof. I recognized my father's smiling face, looking young and happy. I saw odd-shaped houses and strange, misshapen plants, and in one, a twisted, melted glass bottle. But nothing in the box lived up to the delights I had imagined.

Just as I was beginning to lose interest, I opened a large folder that held an eight-by-ten-inch black-and-white photograph of the head and shoulders of a man in a white uniform. He looked just like my older brother John, tan and handsome, with dark thinning hair combed straight back. The resemblance was so strong that I decided to take the picture with me when I left the basement.

After dinner that night I waited for my father to go into his office, where he and my mother shared a desk and a set of filing cabinets. The room was always cluttered with broken chairs, torn clothing, and discarded toys. My father often made phone calls from this room after supper. My mother used it late at night when we had gone to bed to pay bills or make entries in a black book that held the income and expenses of their lumber, coal, and hardware business.

I stood in the doorway until he finished making a call. Then he turned and asked in a kind voice what I wanted. With the photograph in my outstretched hand, I said, "I found a picture of a man this afternoon. It looks like John." My father looked at the man's face and his expression grew sad and worried. "It isn't *your* brother John. This is *my* brother John. He was killed in the war." Before I could ask any questions, he said, "Where did you get it?"

When I answered truthfully his face reflected something I had never seen — a mixture of anger and pain. In that instant I thought he might either cry or shout at me. He chose anger. He rose and walked quickly past me and out the door, yelling, "You kids leave my things alone. Leave them alone." And he was gone. I stood as if I had been turned to salt like Lot's wife. I could not move; I could only stand there and cry. My mother came into the office and asked me what had happened. When I told her, she said gently, "Your father had an older brother named John. He was killed ten years ago. Your father doesn't like to talk about it. Please leave his things alone." Which is exactly what I did.

2

LEAVING HIS THINGS ALONE was easy. Leaving his life alone proved impossible for me, even though my father was one of those men who spent little time discussing his past and even less contemplating past events. He could not have cared less about his mysterious genealogy and would turn away questions about his mother or father or grandmothers or grandfathers with a simple "I don't know." His children were left to guess or to ask someone else in the family who might have answers.

Knowing the answers matters. Understanding the lives of our parents helps us understand who we are. Names, dates, and places accumulate slowly and acquire focus. Suddenly we know what it might have been like to have

been them. And with that knowledge we are more likely
to know ourselves.

Though our memories are different, my father's life
and mine were a lot more closely connected than I had
assumed was the case. Nebraska-born anthropologist and
naturalist Loren Eiseley told of a way to get at these early
memories. His friend, the poet W. H. Auden, once asked
him a simple question: "What was your first memory of a
public event?" Auden believed you could learn a lot about
a person by his answer. My first memory of a public event
was the 1949 World Series when Casey Stengel's New
York Yankees defeated the Brooklyn Dodgers. And I remember China becoming Red China that same fall.

If my father's first memories occurred at the same age
as mine, they would probably have been of Jack Demp-
sey's surprise defeat of Jess Willard for the heavyweight
boxing championship on July 4, 1919, and of Cincinnati
beating the Chicago White Sox in the World Series. And
he must have remembered American troops returning
from World War I.

My father's cousin told me of her uncle's homecoming in 1919: "I was standing in the kitchen with my
mother and I heard her let out a scream. 'He's home,' she
said. 'He's walking up the road.' I went to the porch and
saw this strange man in a brown army uniform looking
very dirty and very hot. It was my mother's brother but he
wasn't the same. He would not sleep in the house. My
mom made a bed of straw for him in the barn. He wouldn't

remove his leggings or help with the farm. In the fall he moved to Ann Arbor, where he worked for a casket maker and lived alone the rest of his life."

In my life the important public events in 1949 centered on the early days of the Cold War. In my father's life the important event in 1919 was the negotiations taking place in Versailles, France. Versailles made both of our lives radically different. The First World War, which began unnecessarily, ended prematurely in November 1918 without a decisive military victory. Instead of destroying the German military and providing the stability needed for the creation of a new order, the great powers were exhausted by the unprecedented destruction inflicted by new weapons against old strategies and driven by the desire for vengeance. The result was isolationism and reparations, a deadly and tragic combination especially since the world was rapidly moving away from the old order of monarchies and colonial power to a new order of nationalism and self-determination.

The Versailles peace agreement and the passionate desire to return to normalcy led America and the other great powers to set the stage for a second world war worse than the first. Rather than preparing for a new age of prosperity and peace, they enabled the rise to power of two of the world's most evil leaders: Adolf Hitler and Joseph Stalin. They also set the stage for the bloody wars of liberation from colonial rule, including the war in Vietnam.

The point of all this is clearer to me today than it was

in 1954 when I learned my father had an older brother. That was the year after Joseph Stalin died and the Korean conflict ended. It was the first year in six that my New York Yankees did not win the World Series. It was the year my youngest sister was born. She was the last of seven and part of the great postwar baby boom.

And 1954 was the second year of President's Eisenhower's first term. Dwight David Eisenhower was the first politician I heard my parents praise, and they even wore I LIKE IKE buttons. Perhaps they liked him because he was from Abilene, Kansas, and his wife, Mamie, from Boone, Iowa. Perhaps it was his good-natured strength of character and modest resolve, or perhaps it was because he had been born in 1890 and was a father figure to them both.

In 1954 the United States was fully engaged in the Cold War struggle against communism, a struggle that brought us both glory and shame. Remembering 1954 is to remember the shame. On December 2, the U.S. Senate voted 67–22 to censure forty-six-year-old Senator Joe McCarthy for contempt and abuse and ended the worst excesses of the anti-Communist movement that distorted our political debate, denigrated artistic expression, and debased our foreign policy. Fear of being accused of Communist sympathies made self-criticism rare and fear of being called an extremist made sustained opposition to the tyranny of Communism more difficult.

In 1954 consumers saw a transformation of the meaning of home. No technology changed the way we lived more than television. When I began school in 1948 few Americans had televisions. But in a single generation nearly all of America's over one hundred million households would spend more and more of their leisure time being amused, entertained, and sometimes informed by the new medium. Advertisers were given a powerfully different way to persuade us that we needed a second car, a larger house, more furniture and clothing, and every labor-saving household appliance we could afford. In 1954 materialism was king.

So was organized religion. American families were joining neighborhood churches or synagogues, listening to and making celebrities of Billy Graham, Bishop Sheen, and Norman Vincent Peale.

In 1954 science promised to revolutionize our lives, and for the first time, American children were being injected with the new Salk vaccine to kill the deadly poliomyelitis virus and end one of the great scares of my childhood. Ours would be the next-to-last generation to be vaccinated against smallpox. Even the test of a hydrogen bomb at Bikini Atoll that was hundreds of times more powerful than the atom bomb thrilled more than frightened us. The launch of Admiral Hyman Rickover's nuclear-powered submarine, the *Nautilus*, showed us how nuclear power would improve our lives.

If materialism governed our homes and the churches our spirit, engineers ruled over the difficulties and inconveniences of Mother Nature. There was nothing they could not do. You say a river is flooding your home or business? No problem, we'll design and build a dam that will generate electricity to boot. You say the slow pace of the two-lane highway cramps the style of your high-compression engine? No problem, we'll build a network of high-speed, high-volume highways from one end of America to the other.

But not everything was calm and peaceful in 1954. Out beyond the shores of my life, tidal waves were forming. On July 21 France accepted defeat in Indochina and signed a peace agreement in Geneva with Vietnamese guerrilla leaders that partitioned the country in two. The United States, which for four years had provided nearly eighty percent of the military support to the French, did not sign the agreement, nor did the government of South Vietnam.

A second tidal wave formed on May 17 when the U.S. Supreme Court ruled 9–0 against the school district of Topeka, Kansas, and overturned the fifty-eight-year-old "separate but equal" doctrine that allowed Topeka and every other school district in America to maintain schools that segregated black and white children. No longer would that division be allowed. "With all deliberate speed" the highest court of the land ordered us to change. The change would be traumatic, deadly, and good.

In 1954 neither the negotiations in Geneva nor *Brown v. Board of Education* had any impact on me. Had they, I would not have considered them as important as say the merger of Hudson Motor Car and Nash-Kelvinator, which meant the death of one of my favorite cars, the Hudson Hornet.

Much of this history I began to understand during a search I set out on thirty-four years after my father told me to leave his things alone. I was a candidate for the U.S. Senate and my father was dying of cancer. He told me his brother John had disappeared during the Second World War. He was officially recorded as dead, but his body had never been recovered. My father told me he was unsure of the circumstances and asked me to find out what had happened. I promised him I would try.

As I searched, I discovered many things I should have known before and many I wish I had known. I've learned that the most daunting of the barriers between us and the truth is this: the hard work of learning something new can bring about the need for personal change, compelling us to think differently, to believe differently, and to behave differently.

My effort to remember has taken me beyond learning about the circumstances of my uncle's death. I've also learned about his birth and life and explored the circumstances of my own. To understand those circumstances, I first need to tell a few stories my father never did.

3

M Y GREAT-GRANDFATHER Thomas Kerry was born in
1830 in the village of Trieshon in Caythorpe Parish
in Lincolnshire, on the northeast coast of England. His
father was the town miller and his mother an ordained
Methodist minister. Frances Reynolds was born in 1832 in
the village of Stoke On Trent, Lincolnshire. Thomas and
Frances were engaged in 1851, the year Thomas, two of
his brothers, and a sister came to America. Frances sailed
alone more than a year later. She and Thomas were married in Boston in 1853.

From there they went to Galena, Illinois, where a girl
and two boys, Harry and my grandfather John, were born.
It was here my great-grandfather added the extra "e" to
our name. When the Civil War began in the spring of

1861, Ulysses S. Grant was working in his father's leather store in Galena. Grant, a West Point graduate and veteran of the Mexican War, was made a general by the governor. Thomas Kerrey volunteered and served under Grant for one year. After his discharge, Thomas and his family moved to Manistee, Michigan, a primitive new lumber mill town. Thomas found a lucrative position in a big mill. Frances raised the children and was active in church and the social life of the town. In 1863 Thomas answered the call of his adoptive country a second time. He raised a company of volunteer soldiers, was made their captain, left his family, and went to war. When he returned, he moved his family to an uncleared homestead in the Michigan woods south of Manistee and built a large timber house. Frances knew nothing about farm life. There were no neighbors other than wild animals, including an abundance of bears and wolves. Harry and John helped with the clearing and planting, and in a few years a splendid farm developed. Frances helped establish a school and throughout the rest of her life she cared for the sick, helped conduct funerals and weddings, and kept the school going. She had three more boys and a girl. Of their seven children only Harry did not manage to complete his education. In addition to farming, Thomas operated a lumber mill in the nearby village of Thompsonville until a spinning saw blade threw a board into his right shin, shattering the bone. His attempt at setting the bone himself failed and he never regained his health.

My grandfather John moved to Chattanooga, Tennessee, where he opened a furniture store. He married Annis Potts, a forty-one-year-old childless widow who bore a son, John Marley, on September 24, 1911. Annis, a diabetic, was warned by her doctor not to have a second child, but on November 23, 1913, she delivered my father at home. They named the boy James and prayed for Annis's recovery. But she bled uncontrollably, grew weaker and weaker, and never left her bed. She held on for more than two months, but according to the notes of the attending physician, on a cold February night in 1914, my grandmother's lungs filled with fluid and she suffocated. The diagnosis was toxemia of pregnancy, a common and often deadly condition that claimed many women before the discovery of antibiotics.

My grandfather was crushed by her death and particularly by her dying wish to be buried with her first husband in Mississippi. He did not believe he could raise the boys alone. Nor did he believe his marriage prospects were favorable. He refused the offer Annis's family made to take the boys and would not even consider an orphanage. His only hope was his sister, Frances.

Frances Potter was born on September 16, 1860, three days after the birth of General John J. Pershing. She was teased about being his secret sister, after Pershing became famous. She married Erastus Valentine Potter when she was nineteen. She raised five children: Jessie, Percy, Raymond, Sena, and Eva. Her husband Erastus died of tuberculosis while staking a claim on farmland in Idaho on November 11, 1913, two weeks before my father was born.

Frances Sarah Potter, or Fannie as she was called, moved back to Michigan following the death of her husband. She was living with three grown daughters and her mother when John told her of his wife's death and asked if he could bring the boys north so she could help care for them. Fannie had just raised all her children and was reluctant, but in the end she agreed. So my grandfather sold his furniture store, packed the boys onto the train, and headed north. A year later he caught a chill and died, Fannie believed, of a broken heart.

In 1914 Fannie was fifty-four, a short white-haired woman with pink cheeks, blue eyes, an avid interest in books, and a determination to raise the boys right. She kept her waist-long hair tucked away in a sensible bun. She had an active mind and a strong belief in hard work. She had collected a small library and expected the children to read along with her. She kept up on the news and politics of the day, had strong opinions, and was an avowed Republican who loved Teddy Roosevelt and disliked Woodrow Wilson. She lived her beliefs and did not waste things, especially her feelings. To her, even birthday celebrations were excessive extravagances. Fannie was the person people in the family went to talk to when they had trouble.

My father loved Fannie and called her Mother. But he felt he was an outsider who never quite belonged in somebody else's family. Fannie had strict rules, such as when they should eat and when they had to study. She also had a sense of humor and loved to tease. Will Rogers was one of her favorite people. She had asthma, which became worse after she and the boys moved to Chicago in 1916, where her daughter, Jessie, taught school and could help Fannie support her nephews.

Chicago was a difficult place then. The streets were violent and Fannie worried over the safety of John and Jim. One of her daughters remembered that Fannie kept the boys in the apartment as long as she could, but when the heat and their energy conspired to overwhelm her, she would descend the stairs slowly, wheezing all the way. Outside she would let John run around freely. She tied Jim to a tree with a piece of cord that limited how far he could go. Then she sat on the porch and watched them both.

The four of them lived in a one-bedroom, third-floor apartment near the University of Chicago. The boys slept on a small porch. They went to Ray Elementary School just six blocks from their apartment, and Jackson High School, a bus ride away. John rebelled and regularly got into more trouble than his shyer younger brother, who lacked John's self-confidence and bravado. They were very close, and John acted as Jim's protector and guardian.

I try to imagine what life would have been like for these two boys in Chicago and how those early memories affected them as adults. It was a time of great change. Mass production of the automobile and the spread of the radio altered people's attitude toward the world around them. In *One of Ours*, Willa Cather's Pulitzer Prize–winning novel, a Nebraska farm boy leaves home for the war in France in 1917. The book tells how the land was farmed fence row to fence row in order to produce food for Europe and how farmers finally decided the time had come to replace their horses with tractors. Millions of horses were slaughtered during the Great War and replaced with hundreds of thousands of more efficient tractors. As a consequence, agriculture and the lives of farmers were radically altered. I once heard Warren Buffett say that if horses could vote, this never would have happened.

Change altered communications. Before the First World War, communication meant the telegraph. Radio was not yet broadcasting the events of the day, but by 1920 people in Chicago heard on their radios the news that Ohio's Senator Warren G. Harding had been elected president of the United States.

As an adolescent John became more difficult for Fannie and Jessie to handle. There were plenty of opportunities for him to get into trouble. Nightclubs and speakeasies were popping up everywhere, and sex magazines and explicit motion pictures were easily available. The temptations were endless. John was adventurous and independent. He stayed out late and too often ended the night with a fight. Fannie began to talk about his need for a man's discipline.

My father was better behaved. I once asked him what

was his happiest day as a boy, and he said it was the day he bought a new pair of boots with money he'd saved delivering the *Chicago Tribune*. Another of his prized possessions came from delivering papers. On his bike route he got to know a local merchant, an elderly Chinese grocer. They became such good friends that on John's tenth birthday the old man gave him a dictionary, which my father carried with him to college.

Both John and Jim liked going to the beach on weekends and to museums, particularly the Museum of Science and Industry. Both witnessed gunfights and beatings, and one crime in particular was seared into my father's memory. Richard Loeb, an eighteen-year-old University of Michigan graduate, and Nathan Leopold, a twenty-one-year-old University of Chicago law student, were sons of wealthy and respected Chicago Jewish families. In the summer of 1924 they committed what they called "the perfect crime": the kidnapping for ransom of a fourteen-year-old boy named Bobbie Franks. All three lived in the Hyde Park neighborhood near Jackson Park, where my father and his brother played. My father remembered every grisly detail of this case: how strongly anti-Semitic feelings ran in the community, and how his older brother had earned a sharp rebuke from Fannie when he repeated a slur he heard at school.

The murder was planned with brilliance, but the perfect crime failed because Leopold dropped his glasses beside the body. Less than a week after the murder, the two were arrested and confessed. Clarence Darrow led the defense and succeeded in getting life sentences instead of the death penalty demanded by the public. My father told me what Darrow said when he almost refused the case: "I was sixty-eight and tired of standing on the thin and lonely line that separates the good from the most destructive force in America: public opinion."

My father had fond memories of the summer pilgrimages north where cooler temperatures eased Fannie's asthma. Fannie's son, Percy, drove them all up in his car to a cabin on an island in Solon Springs, Wisconsin. Percy had a piano hauled up for his wife who played and sang for them all. Many nights Jim and John sat on the dock listening to the adults make music in the cabin while the loons made music on the lake.

They learned to swim, fished together on the dock, and explored along the railway tracks. Each morning they rowed a small boat a half mile to the mainland to collect the mail. Sometimes John impressed his little brother by swimming over and back as Jim rowed beside him.

In Chicago on the afternoon of September 11, 1926, my father suffered one of the worst events of his life. That afternoon John did not show up in front of the building for the walk home, as was their custom. Jim had to navigate the tough neighborhoods on his own and was greatly relieved when he finally reached the safety of the apartment. He ran up the stairs and flew into the room asking Fannie if John was home yet.

"No, he isn't home," she said. "I have sent your brother away for school. I think it's best."

Fannie believed that John was unmanageable because there was no man in the house. On the advice of a friend, she decided to send him to Wentworth Military Academy. Fannie had pulled John out of school and sent him by train to Missouri. It was the saddest day of Jim's childhood. John had always been there, and now he was gone.

John only stayed a year at the military academy. He returned to Chicago in the fall for his sophomore year at Parker High but he was still too much for Fannie. She persuaded her sister, May, who had married Will Mitchell, a prosperous grain merchant, in Duluth, Minnesota, to take him into their home. They lived in a luxuriously paneled house on a large lot in the best part of town. The Mitchells were well enough off to have servants wait on them at supper, an experience John never imagined.

The good times were about to end. The grain business was in trouble and would soon collapse. To make bad matters worse, Will Mitchell was diagnosed with incurable cancer the summer after John arrived and died shortly thereafter. Within months May had lost everything: her husband, her wealth, and her home. She moved her children into a small apartment down by the harbor and was fortunate to find work pumping gas and managing a service station.

John stayed in Duluth, moving into the home of one of his classmates. I imagine him standing on the shore of

Lake Superior early in the evening of June 5, 1930, the day before he would graduate from high school, watching the sun drop below the dark pines on the hills behind the city. Harbor business would normally be booming in the port of Duluth. But he was an experienced enough observer to see that the Depression had already slowed the loading and unloading of grain and iron ore barges that was going on below.

He thought about his prospects for the future. His year at the military academy had been wasted, but he had done well since coming to Duluth. His high school grades were good, especially in mathematics and science. He liked poetry and had written a few stanzas. He hadn't made a lot of friends, but was well enough liked and respected despite his temper.

He wanted to go to college, but having failed to earn a scholarship, he took the civil service examination and scored the highest in his group. But government jobs were just as scarce as jobs in the private sector. He worked through the summer in a Duluth dance club, but when it closed in the fall he was unemployed again. He knew he would be a financial burden on the Mitchells if he remained in Duluth.

In November 1930 John hit the road, looking for work. Like many others, he became a hobo, riding the rails and hanging out in the hobo camps. Or at least that is what the family guessed happened to him. Except for an occasional letter, they didn't hear from him for two and a half years.

When John set out on his own Jim was beginning his junior year at Parker High School. He was doing well and knew from his brother's experience that his only hope for college was to earn a scholarship. He succeeded. In the spring of 1932 he was offered full tuition, room, and board at both Loyola University of Chicago and Iowa State in Ames. He chose Iowa State because Fannie's son, Percy, lived just down the road in Des Moines.

John returned to Duluth in May 1933 because Mrs. Mitchell somehow persuaded the local Civilian Conservation Corps (CCC) to recommend him for a job. He joined thousands of others who exchanged their labor in Michigan's forests for a job, room, board, self-respect, and thirty dollars a month if they promised to send twenty-four dollars home. To get into this program — which Roosevelt signed into law twenty-seven days after his March 4 inauguration — you had to be male, a U.S. citizen, unemployed, between the ages of seventeen and twenty-three, free of venereal disease, and have "three serviceable teeth, top and bottom."

John's CCC work lasted a year. Afterward he moved to Evanston, Illinois, where Fannie's youngest daughter, Sena, and her husband, Cliff, lived. John and Cliff set up a home-based business manufacturing quality hairbrushes. Sold all over the country, the brushes in the end proved too expensive for Depression-era tastes and the business folded.

In 1936, John joined the army, which had a program that paid part of a man's tuition if he committed to active duty after four years of college. John enrolled at the University of Minnesota to study civil engineering. He worked in the cloakroom of the student union and at other odd jobs that came his way.

In 1936 Jim began his studies at Iowa State. In the spring he met a girl in church named Elinor Gonder, who was born and raised near Boone, Iowa, on a farm owned by her parents, Emmett and Josephine. The seminal event of Elinor's childhood occurred when she was twelve years old, and the principal came into her classroom and asked to speak to her. She was an exceptional student and could not imagine this interruption meant anything but bad news. At the railroad crossing in town, her father, who was nearly deaf, failed to hear the oncoming train as his car crossed the tracks. He was hit from the left, crushing his chest. He was still alive when the principal told Elinor the news, but before she arrived home he died.

Her mother could not run the farm alone so she moved her four girls and two boys to Des Moines, found a job working for a credit union, and married a man twenty years her senior. These changes did not slow Elinor down. She graduated at the top of her high school class and won a scholarship to Iowa State. She majored in home economics, but poetry and theater attracted her most. She read all the current books. Pearl Buck's *The Good Earth* made Elinor long to travel, and she dreamed of being alone in a foreign land.

She was a woman with considerable self-confidence. At five feet five inches tall and 135 pounds she had the build of a farm girl. Her large thighs and hips were life-long targets of her self-deprecating humor. Her teeth were crooked and she was nearsighted, which caused her to squint at the world. Her thick auburn hair had a natural curl, and her eyes were a radiant blue.

My father was over six feet tall and handsome with sandy brown hair combed straight back on his high fore-head. A dashing photograph from his college days shows him in a sweater and white shoes leaning casually against the fender of a Ford. Another photograph taken about the same time also reveals how thin he was; he could not have weighed much more than 130 pounds. When my father saw my mother it was love at first sight. He knew this was the woman for him, but she was engaged to a boy from high school. When that boy died a year later, my father seized the opportunity and never let go.

They were not a perfect match. He had Fannie's emo-tional reserve; she was outgoing and expressive. A year after they met, she invited her family to the college to meet her new boyfriend. She and my father stood together on a hill facing the road on which her family would arrive. When the black Ford pulled up, my mother ran down the hill happy and excited. "We hugged, squealed, and jumped up and down with delight," she later said, "but when I turned around to look for your father, he had gone. My emotional outburst frightened him off. I never made that mistake again."

My mother finished college a year ahead of my father and found a position teaching home economics, drama, and English in a high school in Prescott, Iowa. Though she liked the job, it was a long way from Jim. She had more time for books and read Pearl Buck's latest, A House Divided, and James Farrell's Judgment Day, which she liked because it took place in Chicago.

My father was distracted by her absence and his grades suffered, but he managed to graduate in the spring of 1937. His first job was keeping track of time cards at Swift's packinghouse in Chicago. My mother joined him in Chicago, beginning a course in institutional management at the Wabash YMCA. By the fall she had decided the restaurant world was not for her and went back to teaching high school in Indianapolis.

They were married in Indianapolis in October 1938. John was sorry that he couldn't make it because of his studies and his job. All the carefully made wedding plans were upset when my dad and his relatives stopped to pick flowers on the drive down and arrived in Indianapolis after the clerk's office closed. My mother had to track the clerk down in a café to get the certificate. There were one hundred guests, mostly schoolteachers. They held their wedding supper in a restaurant and spent their honeymoon in a hotel on Saturday night. They both had to be back at their jobs on Monday.

In the spring they moved to Waterloo, Iowa, where they set up housekeeping in a two-room, second-story apartment, and my father tried without success to sell insurance. They were strapped financially but they were happy. Their first baby—a boy named Jim after my father—was born that summer. It was a difficult birth and my mother feared her son had been damaged by the doctor's clumsy use of the forceps. In her journal, my mother said she loved having children but not as much as my father did. She was willing to stop working when the babies started coming, but she never extinguished the fire that burned to do more.

4

JOHN FELL IN LOVE at college, too. Her name was Evangeline Mella, and when he first saw her she was sitting with her friends in the student union. John was clearing tables when he heard her laugh and turned to follow the ring of her voice. She had dark wavy hair and brown eyes. She looked like the actress Claudette Colbert, and when he saw her, his heart rose to his throat. He stood there in his white work pants and shirt and looked directly at her. She stopped talking and returned the look. Their eyes met with the intimacy of two people who had known each other a long time.

Days later he saw her again on campus and introduced himself. Her friends called her Vangie, she told him. She was younger than John, and the eldest daughter of five children. Her father was a doctor, an army career officer who had fought in the Great War. Her great-grandfather had helped runaway slaves through the Underground Railroad, and Dr. Mella had named her Evangeline after the character in *Uncle Tom's Cabin*. She had chosen the University of Minnesota because her father was the administrator of St. Paul's Veterans Hospital. Vangie stayed when he was promoted to a position in Washington, D.C.

Constantly together, she and John became an item. He was the love of her life, and she was the balm that calmed his anger. At Vangie's graduation in June 1939, she and John talked about marriage and a family. Under the terms of John's contract with the army, he had to go on active duty before he could finish the fifth year of his engineering degree. Beginning in June 1940, John would have to serve two years, then he could come back to college. They decided to postpone marriage until he had met his two-year obligation. Vangie enrolled in graduate school at the university in order to be with him during his fourth year at Minnesota and while he was in training in the army.

They had to know how precarious their situation was. One year had passed since the Munich conference where Britain, France, and Italy gave Germany license to occupy part of democratic Czechoslovakia. On September 1, 1939, Germany invaded Poland. Appeasement had dissolved into war. In November Finland fell and in April

1940 Germany attacked Denmark and Norway, and then swept across the Netherlands and broke through weak French defenses. By June, when John was leaving the university, German troops were in Paris and three hundred thousand British, French, and Belgian soldiers were being evacuated from Dunkirk.

John was put on orders to the Philippines. Just before he left, he and Vangie drove to Waterloo, Iowa, to visit my mother and father. They arrived ten days after my parents had their second baby, a son they named after John. By then my father had also enlisted in the army and had orders to report to Jefferson Barracks, Missouri, in November. It was the last time my father would see his brother alive.

From Waterloo John drove Vangie across the country to her parents' home in Washington, D.C., stayed a week, and embarked by train for San Francisco, where he would board a ship bound for Manila. After John's train pulled out, Vangie was the last to leave the empty, silent platform. Standing under a single incandescent bulb shining down from an iron pole painted emerald green, she could still hear the last of the laughter and the rustling of clothes as men and women embraced and said their tearful goodbyes. For the first time that day she noticed the cold and was glad she had worn her gray woolen coat and crescent-shaped hat. She pulled mittens from her pocket and slid them slowly over each hand, then her father took her arm and walked her back to his car.

Assigned to General Douglas MacArthur's headquarters in Manila, John found a casual attitude toward the defense of the islands. The Americans and their Filipino allies should have been better prepared for war. In July 1941 President Roosevelt had stiffened American opposition to Japan's aggression in China and Indochina by freezing all Japanese assets in the United States. At a September conference in Tokyo, the United States refused to lift the embargo, setting the stage for war.

On December 7 Japanese aircraft attacked the American naval base at Pearl Harbor and destroyed much of the American fleet. John and other officers on MacArthur's staff struggled to assess the meaning of the attack. They knew it meant war for them. Their world had changed and all their personal plans were put on hold. The battle was drawing nearer to Manila.

The next afternoon Japanese fighter bombers attacked undefended American aircraft on the ground at Clark Field, the U.S. command post in the Philippines. MacArthur's air commander had sought permission to fly his planes so they would be less vulnerable, but the general had refused. Two days later the Japanese landed troops on northern Luzon. On December 22, one hundred thousand Japanese went ashore at Lingayen Gulf. On Christmas Eve the American forces and their Filipino allies began to evacuate Manila for the Bataan Peninsula across the bay to the west. The Japanese occupied Manila on January 2.

General MacArthur had not prepared for a prolonged defense of Bataan. His troops did not have enough food, ammunition, or medical supplies to hold out for long. John and the other surviving defenders lasted four months against superior forces. But on April 9, John and his fellow soldiers surrendered to General Yamashita.

The next day the exhausted, dehydrated, and dysentery-ridden prisoners were forced to march up the peninsula. They did not know their destination or fate. The April heat and humidity were stifling. Drinking water was in short supply and food rations almost nonexistent. The Japanese soldiers were young and poorly trained. They had orders to kill all stragglers, which they did with exuberance and cruelty. Thousands of Americans and Filipinos lost their lives on the march.

After Bataan fell there was one last stronghold held by U.S. and Filipino forces: Corregidor, an island fortress that guarded Manila Bay off the southwestern tip of Bataan. General Jonathan Wainwright surrendered this garrison along with ten thousand American troops on May 6.

Vangie was still at the University of Minnesota when the Japanese invaded the Philippines. She followed the events in the news but heard nothing from John after December. When Bataan fell she still held out hope, but after Corregidor she feared the worst.

In June 1942 Vangie joined the Women's Auxiliary Army Corps. She wrote the War Department asking for information about John and received a curt reply: "The records show that Lieutenant Kerrey is on duty in the Philippine Islands." The War Department had been receiving reports of serious illnesses or casualties, the letter went on, and it "may be of some comfort to know that Lieutenant Kerrey has not been so reported."

She could only guess that John was among American prisoners on the Bataan death march. Vangie heard reports that the men who survived the march and ended up in Japanese captivity were victims of savage brutality. She also knew that some Americans were packed into "hell ships" bound for Japan, where they were sent by train to Manchuria to work in factories that produced war materiels.

In June John was officially classified as missing in action. His name did not appear on the list of prisoners. Vangie believed he had escaped and was alive. "If anybody could survive on his own," she told her sister Georgia, "it was John."

My mother and father were in St. Louis at Jefferson Barracks when the Japanese attacked Pearl Harbor and the Philippines. They learned what they could by reading every news account of Japanese advances and American retreats. When word reached them of the surrender of the Philippines, their best hope was that John had been taken prisoner.

In July my father, a captain in the Army Air Corps, got orders transferring him to Miami Beach. According to my mom's journal, Miami Beach became their long-delayed honeymoon. Since landlords had lost the tourist trade because of blackouts and gas rationing, my parents could rent a beautiful furnished house on a bay with two tiled baths, four bedrooms, and a walled-in backyard, "all on an Army lieutenant's pay." In her words, "they soaked in the ocean, lay on lovely beaches, spent long, lazy days in the sun, and continued to worry about John."

By June of 1943, Miami had started to get expensive, and my father requested a transfer. He was ordered to an air base in Lincoln, Nebraska. He went on ahead and in July, my mother, eight months pregnant with her third child, made the trip to Lincoln with her two boys. They found a furnished second-floor apartment in the small town of Bethany. Their third son was born on August 27 at Bryan Memorial Hospital. Because the hospital was overcrowded, the baby was delivered in the former home of the hospital's namesake: William Jennings Bryan. I am that third son.

During their time in Lincoln my parents joined Bethany Christian Church where they were made to feel welcome. A year later, when my father was ordered to the University of Chicago to learn the Japanese language for the expected invasion, he asked one of his new friends to keep an eye out for a business opportunity. My mother and father both wanted to come back to Lincoln after the war.

The second battle of the Philippines began on October 20, 1944, when U.S. forces landed on the northwest coast of the Bataan Peninsula. On January 9, 1945, the United States attacked Luzon by air and sixty-eight thousand Americans landed on Lingayen beaches. MacArthur returned to Manila on February 4. By then the war in Europe was in its final stages. The Germans counterattacked in the Ardennes forest of Belgium on December 16, 1944. President Roosevelt died on April 12, 1945, at sixty-three years of age. U.S. and Russian troops linked up on the Elbe River in Central Europe on April 25, and Hitler committed suicide on April 30. Victory in Europe was declared on May 8, 1945.

My father celebrated VE Day along with hundreds of thousands of others in Chicago that May 8. But he had mixed emotions, because his war was not over. He had no word of his brother except that John was not on any of the lists of released prisoners. And the country was preparing for the necessary invasion of Japan because the Japanese Army would not surrender unless they were ordered to by Japan's Emperor Hirohito.

My father, who expected to be part of the invasion of Japan, hoped the intensified air campaign led by General Curtis LeMay's B-29s would cause the Japanese emperor to surrender. Between March and June, five of Japan's largest industrial cities and later other smaller cities were targets of incendiary raids. The deadliness of these attacks can be seen in one statistic: in the March 9–10 bombing of Tokyo an estimated one hundred thousand people died.

But it would be a bomb of even more destructive power that ended the war. After a July 16 test near Alamogordo, New Mexico, the United States detonated atomic bombs over Hiroshima on August 6 and Nagasaki on August 9. On the tenth of August the Japanese emperor finally surrendered and Japan sued for peace. V-J Day was celebrated on August 14. Two weeks later U.S. forces landed in Japan and began an occupation with General MacArthur as supreme commander. My father went to Japan as part of an occupation rather than an invasion force.

He arrived in Yokohama on December 1, 1945, and he was assigned to General MacArthur's headquarters, where he tried without success to find out more details of John's disappearance. In February 1946 my father drove his jeep to Hiroshima. He stood at the center of the blast and looked at the circle of destruction around him. He walked half a mile before he could identify objects for what they were. He took a photograph of a glass bottle melted by the heat. A mile away he saw the charred frames of houses, their walls and roofs burned away. People continued to live on the fringes of this gray and flattened mass of rubble. They had begun to rebuild. As he returned to his jeep my father's jaw was set so hard that his chin jutted forward. He held his emotions in check until he saw the children, hundreds of children. These are the orphans, he was told, and my father wept with grief. He could not bear the thought of war destroying so many innocent families.

Soon afterward the army sent him confirmation of his brother's death in the Philippines. According to the regulations of the War Department, he was now a sole surviving brother and could request a transfer home. With demobilization already under way, he chose to leave the service for many reasons, among them his first daughter who had been born April 1, 1945. While my dad waited for the paperwork to go through, my mother's younger brother drove her and the kids to Nebraska and helped her find a place to live. The friend in Lincoln who had promised to watch for a business opportunity had kept his word. He paid one thousand dollars for a lumber and coal business that would be my father's for the asking.

5

LINCOLN WAS STILL A young city when our family arrived for good in 1946. In 1851—the year my dad's
grandfather came to the United States—only thirty hardy
souls lived in this treeless prairie. They called it Lancaster
and they dreamed of making a fortune selling salt they had
discovered nearby. But politics not salt made the founders
wealthy when their town was chosen both for the state
capitol, the state university, and the state penitentiary.

In 1946 when our family settled in Lincoln, parts of
the city still had the look of a frontier town. My mother
took a photograph of our family on a Sunday after church
in early spring 1947 that reveals much about the place.
My father stands behind his three boys. In front of us is a
dirt street called Fairfax; behind us is our home. My

mother's shadow falls across our images. Eight-year-old Jim, Jr., is already tall enough to reach a few inches below my father's left shoulder. Five-year-old John's confident head is chin high to his taller brother. I am three years old and my head doesn't yet reach John's shoulder. The left quarter of my face is hidden behind John's right arm, and I'm dressed in wool shorts and a matching jacket. Our baby sister, Jessie, is missing.

My brothers and father wear stylish fedoras; I am wearing a soft felt cap that is too small for my head. John's eyes are uncovered because his hat is back on his head. The sun is in my eyes because my tiny cap brim does not shade me. My brothers are dressed in identical suits with dark, military-style, four-button jackets and matching pants. They wear white shirts without ties and their collars are turned outside the jackets. My father wears a three-piece suit with a tie. His mouth is open and he appears to be talking to my mother. There is a small but noteworthy distance between my father and his children. His arms are at his sides. Jim, Jr., his hands in his pockets, is looking down and seems to be lost in thought. John stands as if defending us, his hands at his sides and a wide smile on his square face. I am watching my mother. My face appears to be asking, "Why are you doing this to me?"

Only a few trees are visible and they have a barren, scrubby look. Our white frame duplex is about twenty-five feet deep and forty feet long. Its pitched roof cuts the square footage of the second floor in half. Our front porch is five steps up from the concrete sidewalk, which is three steps up from the road. No car is in sight, and I would guess my father parked ours in back to avoid the muddy ruts. My parents' dream of a good place to live had come true. The postwar consumer and baby booms were just beginning. Their prospects had never been brighter.

Our neighborhood was in the northeast quarter of the city. We lived in a village called Bethany that had a block-long business district within walking distance. It contained everything we needed: a doctor's office, a drugstore, a grocery store with a butcher, a lumberyard, a barbershop, and a library. Between our house and the business district was Bethany Grade School. To the north of the shops stood the building that was the center of my parents' lives: Bethany Christian Church.

Every Sunday morning the whole family went to church for an hour of Bible study and another hour of worship. Our congregation practiced full-immersion baptism and shared the belief that Christ was God's son. We learned that human beings are sinners at birth. We believed that Christ's mission was to teach us the way to eternal salvation and that His love was the most powerful force for good. We were taught that Jesus Christ, the son of the living God, died for our sins and that forgiveness was ours only if we declared our belief in Christ. Our family was not enthusiastically religious, but we attended our church regularly and were deeply committed to its community.

The first time I entered the sanctuary of our church I was three years old, and what I remember most is fear. It was large and dark and forbidding. Our family always came in at the back and was met by members of the governing board. After greeting us, one of them would usher us down a side aisle. The sound of our heels hitting the red tiled floor echoed with the organ music. Two sections of dark-stained oak benches were separated by a center aisle reserved for the processional entrance of the minister and the choir, which heralded the beginning of services. Overhead the roof arched into a ceiling high enough to match my imagined estimate of God's actual, invisible size. On each of the sidewalls were six tall, clear, leaded glass windows, which were closed in winter and open in the summer. At the back above the balcony where we sat if we arrived late was a circular stained glass window eight feet in diameter depicting the Virgin Mary, the baby Jesus, and a cluster of attending angels.

Most fearsome to me was the altar in front where the organist played, the minister delivered his sermons from a raised podium, and churchgoers were baptized. An enormous wooden cross hung immediately above the baptismal font. Long after I no longer believed in Santa Claus and the Easter Bunny I still believed this was the cross actually used to crucify Christ.

I held tight to my mother's hand as we were guided to our seats and sat as close to her as possible until the choir entered. With the music came a warm feeling of safety.

My father refused to sit in either the first or the last three or four rows. He preferred a pew a half-dozen rows from the rear. He sat next to my mother, holding her hand or putting his arm around her if she was not cradling a new baby. As we kids grew up our status changed. When we were babies our mother carried us into services. Soon after we could walk we began our Christian instruction in the church basement. When we were deemed ready for baptism, a date would be set for the ceremony.

On my appointed day I got to church a half hour early and entered through the side door next to the minister's office. He gave me a white cotton robe and told me to undress and put it on. Alone in the small bathroom I took off my Sunday clothes and put the robe on over my underpants. I sat on a metal chair in the hallway leading to the baptismal font, waiting for that moment in the services when the minister came for me. While the congregation was singing, he led me down the hallway to the baptismal font, which was hidden on the altar behind a red velvet curtain. He went into the water. The curtain opened and he asked the congregation to stand and join him in welcoming me into the church. Then he motioned to me to come into the water. As I did he reached out, took me by the shoulders, and stood me in front of him. Then he placed his left hand behind my head, turned me so my side faced the congregation, and, offering one last prayer to God, leaned me back under the dark surface of the water and brought me up again. By magic I now belonged to the church. After services I was the center of attention at the potluck lunch served in the meeting hall on the second floor.

Our church service was predictable. At the beginning, the congregation stood and joined the choir in singing the processional hymn. Next came the minister's welcome, followed by a reading of scriptures, followed by another song during which we were allowed to remain seated; then we would stand for the Lord's Prayer and the passing of the offering trays. After the money was collected we sang the doxology. Next came the prayer announcing communion and another song during which six deacons walked down the center aisle to the front. At a small table the minister served them a communion consisting of Welch's grape juice and half-inch cubes of white bread. While the organ played, each deacon picked up a silver tray of small glasses of juice and another of bread. They moved row by row, passing each tray down the pews. Each person took a cube of bread and ate it and drank a cup of juice, taking care to put the tiny glass back onto the tray before passing it on. At the conclusion, the minister offered a final prayer and moved to the podium from which he gave the sermon.

For some time after I was baptized the sermons made no sense to me. Either I sat in perplexed wonder at my parents' ability to understand the droning baritone of our minister, or I offered one of them a chance to play tic-tac-toe in the margins of the church bulletin. The day I first began to understand the meaning of the preacher's sermon, it came as a shock. I was seven or eight years old and felt as if I had penetrated the veil of a secret adult ritual. Afterward I would listen and try to remember every word. Each sermon contained a simple lesson, which could be reduced to a single sentence. This sentence was posted on a sign at the entrance of the church.

Good sermons had quotations from books we all knew we should have read but hadn't. Good sermons had solid beginnings and perhaps funny stories. Good sermons told about poor souls who learned biblical lessons the hard way. Good sermons made sense and stayed with me all week.

After I lost my fear of the church sanctuary I came to love it. It provided my first experience with mystical forces. Sitting in church I felt the presence of God in the sunlight that poured through the leaded glass windows. I would bow my head and know that my prayers were heard. And if I sat quietly and listened closely to the silence, I could hear God's voice telling me what to do.

My heroes came from the stories I heard on Sunday. There were stories about fathers who had spared their children and about men who shared their wealth with strangers. I learned about men and women who had prayed, listened, waited, and then did what God told them to do. I learned that Mary and Joseph had risked ridicule and estrangement from their family and friends to be the mother and father of Christ, the son, who was sent to redeem with love. Christ said, "Whomsoever believeth in me shall not perish but shall have everlasting life." And so I believed.

I also learned heroic stories downtown at the Stuart Theater. Every Saturday morning long lines formed of kids waiting with the price of admission clutched in their hands: a quarter and the severed top of a wax-covered milk carton from the show's sponsor. The Stuart was originally built for live performances, and ornate plaster statues and carvings decorated the walls and ceilings. Pairs of ferocious-looking gargoyles flanked two full balconies with box seats on the sides. A rich purple velvet curtain drew back slowly as we waited eagerly in the dark for the show to begin.

The shows we hungered for were never-ending serials about Tarzan or Zorro or some obscure cowboy character. We remembered every detail of the previous week's episode as we waited breathlessly for our hero to continue his adventures. Each episode closed with the hero trapped and sinking rapidly in quicksand, surrounded by armed bandits or natives, or ensnared in some other life-threatening predicament. We would gasp when the words "continued next week" came on the screen.

The urge to live my life as these heroes did was mixed with the desire to be admired by my peers. I feared their disapproval almost as much as I did that of my father and my older brother, John. By my tenth year I learned how to make my friends laugh by misbehaving and playing practical jokes. I carried on so much in Bible study classes that my teacher made me sit by myself and asked my class-mates to pray for me. I wore this punishment as a badge of honor. I alternated between being a boy clown and a boy drawn to the great stories of the church and to the paral-lel dramas I saw on the Stuart Theater screen.

The other focus of our lives in Bethany was my father's business: a lumber and coal yard three quarters of a mile north of the church. What a wonderful place it was. I can still close my eyes and smell the dry sawdust and freshly cut lumber, hear the whirring whine of the saw, and feel the warm boards waiting to be lifted from a pile of wood. In my early years I seemed to always have a splinter lodged in one of my fingers. Usually I could remove it myself, but sometimes in the evening my mother took my hand and gently, quietly nudged out the wooden dart with one of her sewing needles.

I first met someone from a race other than my own when Wardell Moore, a black truck driver who made weekly coal deliveries in our neighborhood, let me ride with him. He told me he had a son about my age and that he was a good student in school. He taught me how to jump down from the truck at each house and open the door to the coal chute. After a while he even let me handle the scoop shovel he used to push the black nuggets from the front to the back of the truck bed.

Lincoln in the 1950s was about as safe and quiet a place as you could find on earth. Except for the winters, which were hard with freezing winds and punishing blizzards, life was idyllic. Springtime brought floods and muddy roads and lilacs. Summers gave us fireflies, the buzzing chorus of cicadas, the smell of cut grass, and baseball games featuring our Class A team, the Lincoln Chiefs. On hot summer nights when the table fans no longer cooled us, my parents took us outside and spread blankets on the lawn. Sometimes we'd sleep outdoors, telling ghost stories to each other under the stars. When it was sweltering hot and the wind stood still, our father took us for car rides so we could catch the breeze with our hands.

My father loved the freedom our car gave us. Every summer we piled into it for a family trip. At first we traveled in a nine-passenger station wagon, but as we grew we needed two four-door sedans to carry our brood. Each trip was laid out for us on a map provided by the American Automobile Association. My father gathered the family around him and traced the route highlighted in red or yellow. "Follow the line; that's all we have to do," he would say. "No problem." While my father took care of transportation, my mother did all the rest. We ate what she cooked. We slept where she decided and wore the clothes she washed at Laundromats along the way. She organized games and encouraged us to sing songs like "Bill Grogan's Goat" and "I've Been Working on the Railroad" to "pass the time away."

We also found plenty of adventures in Lincoln. Close by our home was a small stream called Stephens Creek where we fished for crawfish and guppies and hid out in sandstone caves. My friends and I rode our bikes to the creek and spent the day exploring and telling stories. We smoked dried stalks of milkweed plants and imagined ourselves as leading men in action movies. We made up stories with ourselves as the heroes who rode in to save the day.

We biked everywhere. The edge of the universe lay at the ends of the dirt roads leading to those places where the wild and woolly frontier began. We were afraid to go farther until one of my friends invited us to his farm. There we got used to the smell of manure and learned how accomplished our farm friends were. They were not afraid of the cows, the horses, or the angry hogs. They knew how a windmill worked, could drive a tractor, and were entrusted with jobs we didn't think kids were capable of doing. I thought they were the bravest kids I knew.

Perhaps they thought we were brave when they spent the night in town. We were not afraid when we ventured out in our neighborhood, day or night. We could stay out until the streetlights came on and not cause our parents worry about foul play. And when we got into trouble and our parents came looking for us, we had plenty of places to hide.

My parents divided the worrying unequally. My mother kept track of all of us. She cooked our meals, cleaned our house, and sewed our clothes. Because of her I learned to play the piano and the trumpet, acquired a respect for the written word, and was given an example of heroic living I could never expect to equal. She was gentle and uncomplaining. In her entire life I knew her to cry only twice: once when she discovered she was pregnant for a seventh time and the other when she caused the untimely death of our cocker spaniel, Rusty, by shutting the garage door on his head.

In 1953 I saw my first television show. The morning of June 2, one of the last days of the school year, my father announced to us that we should come right home to watch the coronation of Queen Elizabeth together. He put the television set in the basement and ran a wire out the window to a makeshift antenna. When I saw the beautiful young queen and her dashing prince, I thought I was witnessing a fairy tale. It could not be real but my brother John assured me it was.

Television, forbidden during the supper meal, became a big part of our family life. Sunday nights we would gather to watch *Gunsmoke, Ed Sullivan,* and *Laugh-In.* We were even allowed to stay up to watch John Charles Daly host *What's My Line?* The struggles of Dorothy Kilgallen, Fred Allen, Arlene Francis, and Bennett Cerf to discover the hidden profession of their weekly guests entertained our entire family.

I carried their famous phrases into conversations with my friends. "Will the mystery guest sign in please?" Or from *To Tell The Truth,* "Would the real _____, please stand up?" I watched Garry Moore smoke one Winston cigarette after another on *I've Got a Secret* and longed to do the same. Popular fashion and culture were my guides to good taste. I listened to AM radio and memorized rock and roll lyrics. I knew every feature of the new model automobiles, dressed according to approved styles, and remained safely inside the circle of public approval.

When I was nine years old I got my first newspaper route. With this job came a liberating feeling of responsibility. I delivered the papers, billed my customers, and collected the money. People depended on me for their news. Every morning, seven days a week, fifty-two weeks a year, I brought seventy or eighty people a folded paper held fast with a red rubber band. On my bike I learned shortcuts and came to know the predawn sounds of a sleeping city, especially the lonesome sound of the trains miles away in the yards west of town. I learned to push on through the mud and rain and snow that often stood between my customers and me.

I had two fears. One was imaginary and the other was real. The imaginary fear came from watching the 1953 movie *Invaders from Mars*. In the movie the Martians lived underground, and unsuspecting victims were seized from below. A hole suddenly opened in the ground, some poor man or woman or kid fell in, and the hole then resealed itself. The Martians could make you disappear without a trace. In the early mornings before the sun rose and I was wrapping rubber bands around my newspapers, a cold chill of terrifying premonition would run down my spine. I was certain the Martians were going to get me.

The other fear was more realistic. Nebraska is a place of flooding rivers. For millions of years we have had floods every spring as the snow melted in the Rocky Mountains and the April showers fell. Engineers built dams and channeled the rivers to reduce their destructive power, but the water still rises in the spring. Once when I was six or seven years old I was in the car with my father when he got caught in a flood somewhere west of Lincoln. Without warning, the water surged and came across the road, blocking our path. He just managed to drive through to safety. I remember looking out the window and down on swirling dark water that seemed oblivious to my life and quite capable of sweeping me away to my death. To this day I am sometimes visited by a dream in which floodwaters threaten my life.

6

THOSE TWO FEARS ASIDE, my hometown seemed the safest place on earth. In my mind Lincoln contained the world's most important people. To me celebrities were the human beings who lived in my neighborhood and who managed through good fortune or tragedy to get their names printed in the newspaper. Outside my neighborhood was the great unknown and unknowable. World events happened somewhere other than my world, where everyone lived forever and no one ever died.

In the summer of 1951, my father asked me to drive with him to Chicago to see Fannie, who was in the hospital. It was my first car trip alone with my father and my first visit to a hospital. The excitement I felt ended when we went into the hospital room where the old woman lay.

She already looked dead. My father pushed me forward and made me give her a ceramic lion I had made in Cub Scouts. It was covered with fake brown fur and painted yellow. I don't remember anything she said, but I remember her very white hair and the blue veins in her hands.

Afterward we drove to the apartment building where he had grown up. We parked in front of the building and walked up to the third floor. Fannie's daughters, Jessie and Eva, invited us in. They had a bedroom where both women slept, a kitchen where Jessie had gone to make iced tea, and a tiny bathroom. The mahogany dining table and the living room furniture were in the same room along with two writing desks overflowing with papers and books. The last room was a screened porch with two wicker chairs and a low wicker table. "This is where your father used to sleep," Eva told me as I explored the place under her watchful eye.

Jessie and Eva were lean, straight-backed women with the same strong hands I had seen on my great-grandmother Frances in the photograph of her churning milk. Jessie suggested we sit in the living room to drink our iced teas and told Eva to turn on the oscillating fan as though running it were a special luxury. I listened to the three of them talk and noted a respect and deference in my father's voice I had not heard before. Though by blood they were cousins to him, these two were his older sisters; to me they would always be Aunt Jessie and Aunt Eva.

He told them that Fannie looked all right. I remember

he said, "She was having more trouble breathing than usual." Our iced teas finished, it was time to go. My dad wanted to make it to Peoria by nightfall so he could reach Lincoln in a single day's drive. Before we left Chicago we drove to the University of Chicago campus. My father stopped in front of Stagg field house. We walked in front of tall gray stone walls that made the building look like a medieval castle. My father showed me a plaque at the entrance that declared it was here on December 2, 1942, that Enrico Fermi and his team had achieved the first self-sustaining chain reaction and had initiated the controlled release of nuclear energy. My father thought I should be impressed that Fermi had done his work in a squash court under the west stands of the football field. But I didn't understand why this place was so important to him.

On the drive back to Lincoln my father told me I would not be working with my brother John that summer. At age ten John was already big enough to drive a twelve-penny nail through a board in two blows. I could barely hold a heavy hammer with one hand, let alone accomplish this superhuman feat. My father knew how big a disappointment this news was to me. I wanted to wear one of the canvas belts the men used to hold their hammers and a supply of nails. I wanted to join them as they hauled two-by-four studs to the foundation of a new house. I wanted to raise the skeleton frame and feel the itch of sawdust sticking to my sweating body.

My father said no. I was too small. As consolation he told me I could help out at the lumberyard and do odd jobs for the shop foreman. When summer came I filled the orders of builders who were putting up dream houses for young families in our growing neighborhood. I learned to mark plywood and lumber with a lead pencil and to hold the wood while the foreman sawed it. I cleaned up and prepared for our next order.

During a lunch break I took out one of the rolled-up paper tubes stored in an empty wooden nail barrel at one end of the table saw. I unrolled it, and as I did inhaled a whiff of ammonia. Inside were white lines on blue paper that I did not understand. I interrupted the foreman as he took a sandwich from his black metal lunch box and asked him about it. He told me it was the drawing for one of the houses my father was building. I was thrilled when he offered to teach me how to read the blueprint.

With one of the stubby wooden pencils that always seemed to be lying about, I began to draw sketches of my own on discarded pieces of lumber. My father, who seldom came into the lumberyard during the lunch hour, surprised us one day with a visit. I didn't see him at first because I was busy with one of my masterpieces. He saw what I was doing and asked what I had in mind. I told him I had picked out a tree in our backyard and wanted to build a house in it. He considered the details for a moment, took the drawing in his hand, and said, "No problem, we can do this." He went back to his office and I stood there wondering what would happen next.

Days later when I had finished supper and was heading out to join my friends, my father asked me to stick around. I followed him into his office. On the desk was a stack of rolled blueprints. My father took the rubber band off one and spread it out before me. The smell of ammonia and the bright blue paper distracted me from immediately realizing what the drawing was. I looked at him, confused, and without a word he pointed to the bottom of the plan where the title of the project was always printed. This one said, "Bob's Tree House." "This will be yours," he said. Had he presented me with a baseball autographed by Mickey Mantle, I would not have been as impressed and happy.

I didn't understand why he decided to reward me but whatever his reason, building this tree house ended my disappointment at not being able to work with my brother. I hauled lumber, held lightweight pieces in place, and even hammered a few nails in my slow and clumsy way. The house was twenty feet square, had a shingled roof, tongue-and-groove siding, and interior walls insulated with rolled asbestos. All four walls had windows, each with a hinged shutter that swung out. There was a door in the floor that swung up and could be fastened with an outside lock. This house was the best thing I had ever owned.

I spent many nights up in the tree, alone and with friends. Few things made me feel as secure as sitting inside my house during a heavy prairie storm. My father had insisted on installing a lightning rod, which seemed silly to me until a bolt hit close enough one afternoon to leave the smell of fire in its wake. Normally what I got from a storm was the sweetest, most intoxicating smell of freshness imaginable.

From this twenty-foot-high perch my friends and I saw and heard things we were not supposed to see and hear, most remarkably, our first look at a fully grown naked woman. Once a week — usually at 2 P.M. on the dot on Fridays — a neighbor lady who liked to sunbathe in the nude came out of her house wrapped only in a towel. My lucky friends and I would climb onto the roof of the tree house at least an hour early, lying and waiting for our world to get turned upside down one more time. We peered down over the edge of the roof breathless and confused about the feelings we were having. She would remove the towel and lay it on the ground. Then she would stand up for what seemed simultaneously the shortest and the longest period of time before lying facedown on the towel. It was as if she were offering herself as a gift to adolescence.

I entered the late summer with a dread of fall because at this age my asthma seemed to have gotten worse. I began to suffer major respiratory congestion and distress. From Labor Day until the first hard freeze, the symptoms progressed and raged on until the morning after the first heavy frost. Then, suddenly, they ended.

While others dreaded the approach of winter and farmers spoke with terror of early frosts, I waited in delighted anticipation for that glorious drop in temperature that would end the life of the annual weeds that tormented me. I wanted what others feared, and feared what they wanted.

The summer before seventh grade was particularly bad for my asthma. Pollen counts were up, the summer was hot and dry, and the excitement of going from Bethany Grade School to Lincoln Northeast High School put me in the danger zone. To say I was excited about going to the high school would be a misstatement. Fear is the more accurate word. The only human beings crueler to each other than seventh graders are older students. God help the kid who doesn't fit in.

At the time my brothers and I were sleeping in two bunk beds in the garage. My nighttime coughing attacks and the high-pitched shrieking I made when I breathed were keeping them awake. My mother had enough and called Elmer Hobbs, our family doctor. He said I was anemic and needed a blood transfusion. I was admitted to Bryan Memorial Hospital for a week. Alone in my bed after the time for sleep had come and gone, I listened to the whistling sound coming from inside my chest with each inhalation and exhalation of breath. An intravenous needle led from my little left arm to a tube through which blood passed into my anemic body. I was not frightened. I felt relieved and safe. I could sleep without worrying about keeping others awake, and anything was better than the trauma of walking down the halls of the high school.

Finally my father decided to do for me what Fannie had done for herself: he sent me north. Fannie's daughter Eva had bought a cabin on White Fish Lake near Gordon, Wisconsin. Because the air was cool and the vegetation different, my father thought the change would do me good. He was right. During four weeks with Eva I swam in the lake day and night. I explored the woods alone and picked blueberries for pancakes. I listened to Eva's stories about being a teenager at the dawn of the century, and I slept on a screened porch with the company of loons lamenting their loneliness and the sound of approaching thunderstorms marching like an army toward the roof of our cabin.

My asthma symptoms abated. I put on a few pounds and acquired the brown, wild look that makes adults love and fear twelve-year-old boys. And when my father came to drive me back to Nebraska for the start of seventh grade, he challenged me to swim across the lake to an island and back, a distance of about a mile. My older brother John had already done it, and that was motivation enough for me. I covered the distance easily and, with all the adrenaline pumping out of my happy heart, I could have swum it twice.

More than anything I wanted to match my brother John's performance. Without benefit of weight lifting or a bodybuilding diet, he became a six-foot-tall, 190-pound athlete. I grew slowly and could not gain weight no matter what I tried. When he was starting on the varsity football team in his sophomore year I was staring into the mirror at a body that was five feet two inches high and tipped our bathroom scale at eighty pounds with my shoes on.

He was a star and I wanted to be one. The girls loved his muscular body, square jaw, and sensuous lips. I dreamed of capturing their attention, but it was not to be. Not only did I remain small and skinny, but I was also cursed with remarkably slow legs, which would not carry me fast enough to compensate for my size. Worse, the arrival of my wheezing and breathlessness coincided with the beginning of football, the one sport I wanted to play more than any other.

I became self-conscious and shy about my body and tried many solutions. Charles Atlas's picture and his advertisements in *Boy's Life* magazine persuaded me to try his dynamic tension techniques. For hours I would press one hand against the other, shifting my arms up, down, in front, and behind me. With each repetition I dreamed of waking in the morning transformed into the anthropomorphic body of my brother. I noticed no change. I drank milk shakes and ate constantly, but could not turn myself into the man I wanted to be.

Most of my friends were having the same difficulties. Even those friends whose bodies grew fast enough to get them onto the football field or the basketball court appeared to have the same confidence deficit disorder I had. We compensated with rowdy behavior. We soaped windows on Halloween night. We acted up in class. I became a small hero when I was asked to leave my Boy Scout troop after many unsuccessful efforts to design my own merit badges. We started a club in the loft of a friend's garage, which was once a barn. We called ourselves the Angels but we became the Angles after we let our poorest speller write our name on our door.

In the winter the Angles gathered to ice-skate and took chances sliding on a sled tied with a rope to the bumper of a fast-moving car. In the spring we took to the streets, roller-skated, and hung out at a local drive-in restaurant, one of the first of its kind. On occasion we challenged boys at other high schools with attacks on their territory.

Fear of our parents and other adult leaders kept us from going too far with our misdeeds. The most important adult leader of my youth was a man named Harlan Johnson. He organized YMCA camp retreats, athletic activities for those who did not make the high school varsity squads, and unusual events that challenged us in unexpected ways.

During the summer before my sophomore year I spent a week that would affect me much later in life at the YMCA's model legislature. Forty-nine boys were given a chance to learn about Nebraska's legislative process. Each of us represented one of the districts in the Unicameral, the only single-house, nonpartisan legislative body in the country. We went to Nebraska's capitol, the tallest building in Lincoln and easily the most beautiful. There we were assigned desks in the actual chamber used by the real representatives of the people. The political issues we debated were contrived and irrelevant but not in my mind; at the time I thought that what we were doing was important.

My first personal experience with a political issue was when I went to meet a fellow Angle at his home. In a heavy accent his mother told me he had gone to take his driver's test and was on his way home with his father. When she invited me in I hesitated because my friend had made it clear he did not want us to meet his family. I knew the parents of all my friends except his, but he had used every excuse to keep us out of his home.

She wanted to talk and wasn't offended when I asked about her accent. She was from Latvia and showed me where it was on a map. She had come to America because of the Russians. "The Nazis and the Communists. They are the same to me. No difference; I hate them both." I had never met a Communist in Lincoln, but if my friend's mother hated them, so did I. We had been talking in their living room for nearly an hour when my friend walked in. He looked surprised and worried. I had violated his rule and he wanted me out of the house.

We left and drove off in his car. When I asked questions about what his mother had said, he would not tell me anything. He was ashamed of her heavy accent and his father's inability to speak any English at all. It didn't help that I thought he was brave to have been a part of this flight in the face of great danger. As we drove up the tree-lined street we quickly forgot the incident because this was our first ride in a car not driven by an adult. My friend's escape from Latvia had given him one enormous advantage over the rest of us: he was a year older and was driving a full year before we could. He would be much in demand.

One day that summer he drove several of us to an outdoor trampoline center. The trampolines were built so that the springy jumping surface was just above the ground. For twenty-five cents you could have fifteen minutes of acrobatic pleasure. The idea came into my head that I should attempt a maneuver I had tried on a swimming pool diving board: a one and a half somersault. I was confident I could do it. I came around in plenty of time to land flat on my stomach with my arms stretched forward to break the fall. Unfortunately I did not land on the trampoline. I landed on the sidewalk. The blow shattered my front teeth. I sat against the chain-link fence with my hands covering my mouth until my friends had used up their time on the trampolines. Then I went to my dentist who pulled what was left of the teeth.

7

O N JANUARY 21, 1958, nineteen-year-old Charlie Stark-weather and fourteen-year-old Caril Ann Fugate murdered eleven people during a two-day killing spree. Three of their victims were at home in Lincoln. Fear flickered like lightning as word of the violence spread through town. The radio broadcast a warning from school administrators and asked parents to pick up their children at school. My mother took the risk seriously enough to do just that. We all breathed a sigh of relief and went back to our normal lives when the couple was arrested in Wyoming.

In the 1950s we were told that the greatest danger to our freedom was not Charlie Starkweather or Martians or floods or trampolines. It was the threat of the Soviet

Union. The Soviets weren't the kind of danger that would cause a mother to pick her children up at school. We didn't fear a physical invasion, which would drive us from our homes. The conflict with the Soviet Union was more like gravity; it was simply a force that influenced much of what we did and thought.

Our presumption was that the Soviets were at war with us and were determined to conquer us however they could. We were told they were trying to take advantage of our open society by infiltrating our government, businesses, and even our churches. I never met a Communist when I was growing up, but in the rhetoric of the day that was because a Communist would never tell you he or she really was a Communist.

We heard that their centrally planned economy was producing tremendous gains in productivity and standards of living and that their schoolchildren were smarter, worked harder, and were likely to "bury us" unless our attitudes changed. It was traumatic for us when the Soviets launched *Sputnik*, the first artificial satellite to leave earth. And months later when a United States rocket blew up on the launching pad, we took it personally. It meant we were behind, that our scientists and engineers were inferior, that something was wrong with our schools, and that our students weren't as good as Soviet students in the subjects that mattered.

The Red Scare was a real experience in the fifties in Lincoln. The Reds were after our drinking water. They were after our children. President Eisenhower was speaking gospel when he used Joseph Alsop's phrase to justify U.S. aid to the French to fight Communism in Vietnam in 1954. Alsop said, "If you have a row of dominoes set up, you knock over the first one, and what will happen to the last one is the certainty that it will go over very quickly." The year I turned sixteen, Major Dale Buis and Master Sergeant Chester Ovnand became the first and second Americans to be killed in Vietnam.

My memories of most of the great moments of the Cold War are not vivid, but some were too big to miss entirely. I don't remember what happened during the 1948 Berlin airlift that overcame a Soviet blockade of Berlin from West Germany, but I remember hearing others talk excitedly about it. I don't remember the details of Alger Hiss being accused in 1948 by *Time* magazine senior editor Whittaker Chambers of being a Soviet spy, but I do remember something about secret messages hidden inside pumpkins. As I said before I remember the 1949 Communist victory in China, but only as something that happened to China to make it Red. The 1949 Soviet detonation of a nuclear weapon I remember; it was on a newsreel at the Stuart Theater. Senator Joe McCarthy's four years of anti-Communist efforts beginning in 1950 were a remote happening. I did not mark as significant either the death of Stalin in 1953 or the executions of Ethel and Julius Rosenberg that same year.

Some of my memories have come back only after

studying current events of the time. While I do not re-member the invasion of South Korea by the North and heard nothing about the terrible U.S. losses in the sum-mer of 1950 or the stunning success of Inchon, I do remember General MacArthur being recalled. And I remember talking about a *Life* magazine article the fol-lowing spring that told the story of wave after wave of Chi-nese soldiers attacking, seemingly without regard for the terrible losses being inflicted upon them. They had to be different than we were. They couldn't value life the same way we did. It seemed the only reasonable explanation for their behavior.

The same "us-versus-them" attitude carried over into the other great battle of the day: the struggle by black Americans for civil rights. My store of Cold War memo-ries is large compared to the battle for civil justice. *Brown v. Board of Education* overturned the legal principle of "separate but equal" and said in essence that segregation in our schools was a violation of the Fourteenth Amend-ment to the Constitution. It says a lot about my view of the world that I do not remember the day in 1954 this de-cision was announced by a unanimous Supreme Court. The key community represented in the *Brown* case was Topeka, Kansas, 125 miles southeast of Lincoln. And one of the key players was a Nebraska native, Herbert Brownell. Mr. Brownell was appointed Attorney General after he successfully managed President Eisenhower's 1952 cam-paign for president and promised Governor of California

Earl Warren the first slot on the U.S. Supreme Court if he agreed to support Ike.

In our nearly homogenous community, racism was a problem that infected the thinking of other people and not us. Not one black student attended Lincoln Northeast during my six years there. In fact, I didn't have a black classmate my entire thirteen years in the public schools. In part this was because the few blacks that lived in Lincoln were kept out of our neighborhood by discriminatory real estate practices. In part it was because black students were sent to a segregated grade school, though I was unaware of it at the time.

Today, when I read the defense used in 1954 by the Topeka School Board it seems likely I would have shared their sentiment. The Topeka board argued that because segregation in Topeka and elsewhere pervaded many other aspects of life, segregated schools simply prepared black children for the segregation they would face during adulthood. Segregated schools were not necessarily harmful to black children. Great African Americans such as Frederick Douglass, Booker T. Washington, and George Washington Carver had overcome more than just segregated schools. That was the mainstream logic of the time and nothing in my experience would have caused me to question it.

I simply did not know any minorities well enough to realize the kind of barriers they confronted. I had no experience with discrimination and no passion to end it. The only reasonable supposition is that I must have reached the same conclusion as the majority in Lincoln: there was no problem with things just as they were.

I did have one personal connection with problems facing people who were different. My eldest brother, Jim, was born slightly mentally retarded. He had been practically ripped from my mother's body by a young and inexperienced doctor who used forceps without regard for the damage that could be done to a baby's head. My mother thought this violence explained my brother's slowness. His physical development was as rapid as his intellect was slow. Jim grew faster and bigger than anyone in our family, and he didn't stop until he was six feet seven inches tall.

In the same year as *Brown v. Board of Education*, my parents were told Jim could no longer continue in public school. He was doing poorly in his classes, and the system simply judged that trying to help him was wasting taxpayers' dollars. So they sent him home and told him he would not be allowed to return.

The two choices my parents faced were to keep him at home or to find a private school. My mother found a program in Philadelphia that advertised itself as giving special care to children who could not do well in the public schools. They took the train to Philly to make certain the place was on the up and up. They liked what they saw and left Jim there.

This farewell must have been terribly painful for my brother and my parents in a way that I did not appreciate at the time. My father in particular would have been reminded of the ordeal of his older brother. For me my brother's departure wasn't an ordeal. I had other brothers and sisters to keep me company. Besides that, Jim's slowness embarrassed me. I didn't want people to know he was my brother. I was afraid I would be judged by others if they knew he was part of my family.

My brother was not away very long. At first my mom and dad attributed his unhappiness and complaints to his being homesick. "He'll be all right after he makes some new friends," they reasoned. But he didn't make new friends and he wasn't all right. After several months of letters from him describing the poor conditions, my parents decided to check things out for themselves. They found Jim with his head shaved, wearing a uniform that resembled prison pajamas, in a cold dormitory with bathrooms that did not work. On the spot my father decided to take him back to Lincoln.

My parents were as proud of Jim as they were of all their children. They hired a tutor and helped Jim find work. But his physical problems got worse when he began to have seizures diagnosed as epilepsy. Our doctor prescribed Dilantin, but he didn't know that long-term exposure to Dilantin produces alarming side effects, including loss of the blood supply to the mouth. Before this mistake was discovered, Jim's gums atrophied and he lost all his teeth.

People like Jim who are different but who want badly to be liked are vulnerable to abuse. One day in early June of 1960 between my junior and senior high school years, I ran downstairs to my room to change clothes. As I passed Jim's room I saw he had someone with him, a boy in my class who had been hanging around my brother for reasons I suspected were not good.

From my room I listened in on their conversation. I heard the boy ask my brother to lie down on the bed. I heard him say, "My, you sure are tall." Then I heard a rustling of clothes and the words, "My, you are big, too." I rushed into the room. Jim was lying down and the other boy's hands were on him. I told him to leave. Then I made him leave.

Afterward I was angry with myself because his punishment seemed incomplete. A week later I was given a chance to correct my mistake. Late in the afternoon I was driving my father's car when this same boy pulled his car alongside mine and extended his right hand in my direction with a single finger raised. This universally recognized insult gave me the excuse I needed.

He drove into the parking lot of a grocery store and went inside. I parked and waited for him inside the doorway. When he walked by me I hit him before he could raise his fists. I pushed him down and, with my knees on his shoulders, began to bang his head on the concrete. I was way ahead on points when I heard a woman shout, "Police! Call the police!" It seemed like a good time to stop what I was doing. When I looked up I saw one of my teachers. Now I was convinced it was a good time to make my exit.

We both got up. I was ready to leave but the boy was not through fighting. We were in the lawn and garden section of the store, and he grabbed a pair of pruning shears from a display rack. He began making lunging motions in my direction. I had seen some cowboy hero in a movie take a knife away from an attacking foe and I tried to do the same. But instead of twisting the pruning shears out of my opponent's hands I took the blades in my side. Both of us were shocked. My attacker pulled back; he did not pursue the advantage.

I decided the fight was over and ran out of the store unaware of the seriousness of my wound. In the car I realized I needed to visit the hospital. In the emergency room of Lincoln General a doctor stopped the bleeding, and as he was sewing up the incision told me the blades had come a half inch from penetrating my cardiac membrane. As soon as the wound was closed, a sheriff's deputy told me to follow him to his car for a ride to the jail.

There I was surprised to see my attacker sitting at a desk talking good-naturedly with one of the officers. He claimed to be a defenseless victim who had been harassed by me before and who was afraid I would hurt him. He had no idea why I had attacked him. I would not supply the missing piece. The county attorney charged me with assault with intent to do bodily harm and took out a peace bond against me. This meant that if I approached my classmate for any reason the official would file criminal charges. Then he called my mother and father to escort me home.

My father took the side of the law. My mother knew something was up, and she probably suspected what my classmate had done to my brother. She was angry with the county attorney for not listening to both sides of the matter. For me it was a lesson of some significance. My fighting had helped neither me nor my brother. I had embarrassed my family, and I got a brief but lasting look at the law. I did not like what I saw.

Though I wasn't constantly in trouble with the law, I thought the law was little more than a flashing red light in my rearview mirror. The law was there to keep me from doing things I wanted to do: drive fast or disrupt someone's peace at night. My difficulties seemed to grow when I got a car, escalating during the summer.

Saving me from a worse fate was my father's expectation that I would find work when school was out. One of my best jobs during my high school years was with Arnie Bartlett and Ray Watts, who built concrete foundations, slabs, and brick walls. Arnie and Ray were good-natured, a comic pair who could outwork all of the younger men they hired as helpers. They taught me to dig footings, form a slab with plywood, level sand, lay wire and iron bars, and move concrete as it came down the chute of the truck.

Most of the slabs were foundations for silos to store the grain of local farmers or grain elevator operators. We built corrugated steel structures in a dozen or so small towns within an hour's drive of Lincoln. Occasionally we got a job far enough away so we had to put up for the night in a local hotel. Those were the good nights when I shot pool, ate my meals with Arnie and Ray, and worked until the job was done. Though we were never more than an hour from Lincoln, it seemed as though we had gone to the other side of the universe, where I was free from my parents' authority.

8

L IKE SO MANY MEN my age, some of the most important
lessons I learned in school were outdoors on a playing
field surrounded by an oval running track. The Lincoln
Northeast High School track was north of the school's
three-story red brick building, and the field was of little
significance to anyone who never played high school football. For those who have, the sight of two white wooden
goalposts at opposite ends of a hundred-yard field of grass
surrounded by an oval quarter-mile track holds special
meaning.

It is a place where a man can recall an afternoon
or evening of his youth with absolute clarity. Thirty, forty,
fifty years later the memory will still be fresh. For this is
the place where a boy learns as much about the game of

life as he does about the game of football. This is the place where a boy learns that the confidence of a spectacular success is necessary to help him survive the deflation of a brutal failure, which can come on the very next play. It is a place where a boy learns that individual effort must be sustained through mind-numbing fatigue and that helping a team of players to succeed can be a more lasting glory than individual stardom.

I remember some forty-year-old moments as if they just happened. I once made an absolutely perfect block that made the coaches nod at each other in approval and fellow players nod at me with momentary respect. I once tackled a running back with enough force to reverse his forward motion. Practically an entire lifetime later I can hear sounds of that one block and that one tackle and recall the pride I felt afterward. I also remember missed blocks, missed tackles, and everything else in between, which is mostly where I performed.

As a player my contact with greatness was infrequent. In truth the only time I am certain I experienced greatness was as a witness to it. And greatest of all was the memory of playing an afternoon game of football against Omaha Central High School, whose star player was Gale Sayers, who went on to a hall of fame career with the Chicago Bears. We only lost by a touchdown. I played a good game on offense, but on defense I couldn't even touch the hem of Sayers's garment. I was playing right linebacker as he swung wide around his left side, eluded me with grace, and ran seventy and eighty yards for a touchdown.

The first time I suited up for practice was in August 1959, in a storage room next to the gym lockers. We were given plastic shoulder pads and heavy white cotton pants, with hard fiber pads for the thighs and softer pads for the knees. A plastic helmet with a canvas suspension was designed to limit the damage of crushing blows. A single half-inch curved metal bar fastened to either side of the helmet protected against larger objects, such as another player's helmet, but it was no protection against a fist, a forearm, or a kick. We wore black leather, high-top shoes with removable hard rubber cleats.

The only equipment we had to bring to this first practice were three articles of clothing: a jockstrap, a pair of sweat socks, and a T-shirt. Many players never took these items home to be washed until the season was over, and I will never forget the acrid smell of the locker room. It was almost as bad as my uncle Ronnie's turkey coops on my mother's family farm near Rippey, Iowa. The pungent smell in the locker room intensified as the season progressed.

A third of the 150 boys in my class tried out for the football team my sophomore year. On the first day each of us understood there were three possible outcomes: we would quit, we would be selected for the sophomore team, or best of all we would be good enough to make the varsity roster. The sophomore team was the coach's way to give a player a chance to stick around long enough to see if growth or experience would add something that would get him picked for the regular team during his junior year when there were only two options: varsity or no football.

When I left the locker room for the first time and ran to the practice field to face the coaches, I felt dread. My breathing was rapid and a tightness in my chest signaled something worse than physical pain. I dreaded the humiliation of performing poorly in front of others. My nightmare scenario was doing something so foolish, so pitiful that laughter would be my reward. But I also dreamed I would do something that elevated me to the status of legend. Both possibilities battled for my attention. As it turned out, neither became reality. I was assigned to the line coach where determination could make up for deficiencies in speed, size, and strength. And though I did not make the varsity roster I was a regular sophomore starter.

Our young bodies took a beating on the rock-hard bare field where thick grass grows only in the end zones. A few of the scars on my old body tell stories from those days. A pale white line between the third and fourth fingers of both hands came courtesy of the cleats of competitive upper classmen. My knees and elbows were almost always bloody thanks to regular trips to the ground. I have a mark below my lower lip due to having my teeth pushed through the soft flesh following a sharp blow to my mouth.

I will never forget the names of my coaches and how they looked. Our head varsity coach was Art Bauer, a

TOP ROW: Henry, Horace, Mary (Mitchell), John Kerrey, George.
BOTTOM ROW: Frances (Potter), Thomas Kerrey,
Frances Reynolds Kerrey, Frank, c. 1890.
Courtesy of Bob Kerrey

Emmett and
Josephine
Gonder,
unknown date.
*Courtesy of
Bob Kerrey*

Frances Kerrey, unknown date.
Courtesy of Bob Kerrey

Annis Potts, unknown date.
Courtesy of Bob Kerrey

Frances Potter, c. 1920.
Courtesy of Bob Kerrey

John and Jim Kerrey, c. 1924.
Courtesy of Bob Kerrey

Elinor Gonder, 1932.
Courtesy of Bob Kerrey

Jim Kerrey, 1933.
Courtesy of Bob Kerrey

Jim Kerrey, c. 1933.
Courtesy of Bob Kerrey

Jim Kerrey, unknown date.
Courtesy of Bob Kerrey

John Marley Kerrey, c. 1936.
Courtesy of Bob Kerrey

Jim and Elinor Kerrey, 1937.
Courtesy of Bob Kerrey

Bob Kerrey, 1944.
Courtesy of Bob Kerrey

LEFT: Jim Kerrey with John, Bob, and Jim, Jr., 1943.
Courtesy of Bob Kerrey

Jim Kerrey, 1945.
Courtesy of the U.S. Army

Jim Kerrey with Bob, John, and Jim, Jr., 1947.
Courtesy of Townsend Studios — Lincoln, Nebraska

Fifth grade class, Bethany School—Bob Kerrey, bottom row, third from right, 1954. *Courtesy of Evans Photo Studio, Lincoln, Nebraska*

Jim Jr., John, Bob, Jessie, Bill, Sue, and Nancy Kerrey, 1958-59. *Courtesy of Bob Kerrey*

Bob Kerrey, 1960.
*Courtesy of
Evans Photo Studio,
Lincoln, Nebraska*

1960 Lincoln Northeast
Rockets—Bob Kerrey,
bottom row, third from right.
*Courtesy of Evans Photo Studio,
Lincoln, Nebraska*

Bob Kerrey, 1961.
*Courtesy of Evans Photo Studio,
Lincoln, Nebraska*

Bob Kerrey, President
of Phi Gamma Delta,
standing in front of frat
house, 1965.
© *University of
Nebraska Photography*

Bob Kerrey, 1968.
Courtesy of the U.S. Navy

Bob Kerrey with President Richard Nixon, Elinor and Jim Kerrey, 1970.
Courtesy of the Richard Nixon Library & Birthplace

Elinor and Jim Kerrey, 1975.
Courtesy of Bob Kerrey

dark-skinned man in his late thirties whose muscular legs made him look like he could still play the game. Max Hester was Coach Bauer's first assistant. The other was Hank Williamson, who doubled as head coach of the sophomore team. These three did something for me that strengthened my character as much as my parents did. They taught me why I had to fight on no matter how hopeless a situation seemed at the time.

When I was a sophomore my brother John was the starting senior fullback for the varsity squad, as he had been all three years. He was big and fast and was just what the coaches were looking for. I was small and slow and would have to grow some to be noticed. Because I did not make varsity my sophomore year, I did not get to play on the same team as my brother. My junior year I made the team and played enough to earn a letter.

Going into my senior year my goal was to make the starting team. I reasoned I had a fighting chance because in my junior year I played backup to the starting center who had graduated. Now, all I had to do was beat out the third-string kid and hope no one new showed up from the freshman ranks. My dream was to be announced with the starting roster at our first game against one of our crosstown rivals.

We began our practice in late August 1960 before school started. We had two weeks of a schedule known as two-a-days, meaning we practiced twice a day, once in the morning and once in the afternoon. It was cooler in the

morning, and we could do wind sprints and other strenu-
ous exercises without losing too much water. In the after-
noons we were told to take salt tablets to prevent heat
exhaustion or heat stroke.

The heat was nothing compared to my need to add
weight and survive the asthma season. I had gained fifty
pounds since my sophomore year, but still only weighed
155 at the beginning of practice. The previous year I had
noticed that the boy who started at center had trouble
snapping the ball accurately for punts, and I noticed how
critical this relatively simple skill could be in a close
game. I came to my last season having spent the summer
working to master the punt-snap technique. Hundreds
and hundreds of times I snapped the ball at a car tire hanging waist high from a rope on a clothesline pole fifteen
yards behind me. I knew that throwing without shoulder
pads was easier than with them, so I practiced throwing
the ball farther and harder than would be needed in a
game. As my accuracy improved my confidence soared.

Two-a-days began a few days after my seventeenth
birthday. So did the asthma season. My determination to
have my best year on the field collided with unusually
high pollen counts. My body needed every calorie I could
put into it just to deal with the attacks of asthma. The exertion of morning and afternoon practice burned pounds
off me like ice melting in July. Whatever gains I had made
that summer dripped away in the two weeks before our

first game. As that Saturday approached I no longer expected to start. On Friday the roster for Saturday's game was posted on the door of the locker room. I stopped to read the list. Not only had I failed to make the starting team, I had not even made the traveling roster. I would not suit up for the game. The news cut my heart. Tears welled up in my eyes, but I would not cry in front of my teammates. I went straight outside to my bike and headed home. Somewhere in the first few blocks I changed my mind. Rather than face my father—or worse, my brother— with this terrible failure, I decided to face the coach.

I knocked on Coach Bauer's door and asked if I could talk with him. No longer able to keep from crying I bowed my head while I spoke. "Coach, I can't keep trying. I have to quit." Coach Bauer asked me to sit down. He was reassuring. He told me this was just one game. I had worked too hard to quit. He urged me to give it one more try. I agreed.

At dinner that night my father asked about the next day's game. My brother John was sitting across from me. I made certain I did not look him in the eye. I answered that I would not be suiting up but would be on the sidelines. In a cheerful voice my father said, "No problem! You'll make it for one of the games." His optimism did not alter my dismal view of myself.

The next day the team looked terrible. We were favored to win but lost. And the starting center did poorly.

I started the next game and every other game that year. At season's end the bridge of my nose was permanently scarred from the attack of every noseguard I faced. This little scar would remind me how close I had once come to quitting and how much of a payoff there was for perseverance.

9

IN THE SPRING OF 1961 before high school graduation I
decided to go to the University of Nebraska in Lincoln.
I did not consider any other college. The university was
the hometown school where my brother had gone before
me and many of my friends were going. And the pride a
Nebraskan feels for the university — even before our football team became famous — is something that cannot be
understood by residents of states where the college scene
is dominated by a venerable but private institution.

Most of my high school class of more than three hundred did not go on to college. They went right to work in
factories where wages were still high enough to support
their families. There were good jobs at Goodyear Tire and

Rubber, the Burlington Northern Railroad, Western Electric, Cushman Motors, Gooch's Mill, and other smaller manufacturing businesses. Every male knew that two years of military service was required by law, but only if there was a shortage of volunteers. The need for recruits was too small to present any real risk to us of being drafted. The Vietnam War was not much of an issue for the class of 1961.

I chose pharmacology because I loved chemistry and because a university counselor explained how I could complete my pharmacy training in four years by taking a heavy load and going to summer school. That convinced me. I was eager to finish school and get out into the world on my own.

In August before classes began I ventured outside the safety of my hometown for the first time. Three fellow Angles and I drove to New York City. We saw all the tourist attractions—the Statue of Liberty, the Empire State Building, and Ellis Island. We saw Mantle and Maris play at Yankee Stadium. And we went to Greenwich Village where we had our portraits sketched by a street artist and managed to get into the Bitter End for a performance by John Coltrane. We were four square young men from Lincoln, a universe away from the people we saw here. Driving out of New York we laughed at how different everyone in the city was—but knowing that we were the ones who did not belong.

I was beginning to sense that I could no longer remain

outside the flow of world events. Newly elected President Kennedy had said in his inaugural address on January 20, 1961, that Americans were willing to "pay any price and bear any burden" to win the battle against Communism. Two months before I graduated from high school in 1961, he authorized a CIA-supported invasion of Cuba at the Bay of Pigs. And the tensions were not confined to Cuba. In 1960 Soviet surface-to-air missiles had shot down an American U-2 spy plane and captured the pilot, Gary Powers. In August 1961, East Germany closed the border between East and West Berlin and constructed the Berlin Wall. Also in 1961 the Soviet Union detonated a thermonuclear device that was the largest ever exploded; its shock wave was felt around the world.

Around the world four hundred years of Western empires were coming to an end, in some cases peacefully and in some cases not. Colonies in Africa, Asia, and South America were becoming independent nations and some became Cold War battlegrounds. I would not have pretended to understand or care about the underlying nature or history of these conflicts. And as for emotional engagement, compared to the genuine sadness I felt when rock and roller Buddy Holly's plane flew into a snowstorm after a concert in Clear Lake, Iowa, on February 3, 1959, these other events barely registered with me.

When I entered college, I would have done poorly on any test that asked me questions about the origins of our country or about the great narratives of the men and women who built it. I would have done well on a test that asked about the periodic table and algebraic, geometric, and trigonometric problems. I did not understand the history of people, their lives, deaths, successes, failures, destructive ways, and creative abilities. I knew or cared little about the world outside of Lincoln.

I had one girlfriend who went to Alabama with the Freedom Riders in May 1961 just before we graduated. She told me how frightened she was by the police who stopped the bus she was riding in and by the hatred other white people showed toward her. I thought it was brave of her to go but had no interest in joining her.

For a story to reach me it would have to be in a movie theater. I went to most of the new movies that opened in Lincoln. In 1961 they included Jackie Gleason and Paul Newman in *The Hustler*, Stanley Kramer's *Judgment at Nuremberg*, and *A Raisin in the Sun* with Sidney Poitier. I saw Audrey Hepburn in *Breakfast at Tiffany's*, *The Guns of Navarone* with Gregory Peck and David Niven, Marilyn Monroe and Montgomery Clift in *The Misfits*, and Vincent Price in *The Pit and the Pendulum*.

I read what my mother recommended to me. Usually it was a Book of the Month Club selection, her source for books, or something she saw in *Reader's Digest*. In 1961 the only book I read that came out that year was Joseph Heller's *Catch-22*. Beyond that I had no contact with the world of culture. I knew a guy who became a painter, but in 1961 he was too strange for my company. I could not have told a Picasso from a Miró and did not know who Stella, Twombly, de Kooning, Johns, or Warhol were.

My pharmacy courses were mostly in the sciences— chemistry, math, physics, and pharmacology. I especially loved chemistry and its magical color changes, energy releases, and precipitations of newly created substances. In the dark labs smelling of strong acids and bases I learned to test for nitrates, sulfates, and phosphates and to tell which metals were present in various liquid and solid substances. I learned to measure precisely and to record the results meticulously in spiral notebooks that quickly gathered the stains of the laboratory reagents and dyes.

My only liberal arts courses were in elementary philosophy and elementary literature. I barely understood the difference between deductive and inductive logic. I was confused by the arguments, and did not know if I was a fatalist who believed in predestination or a determinist who believed I was the master of my own fate. In English I could not make sense of metaphors or muster excitement for the stories we were assigned to read. The only nonscientific course I remember well is economics, only because the lectures were broadcast from two television sets mounted from the ceiling in the front of a large room; they reliably put me to sleep.

In order to belong I joined a fraternity, Phi Gamma Delta, and lived by its written and unwritten rules. Some of my friends did not because they would not bend to the conformity that dominated every fraternity house. Those

who did not fit in for physical, psychological, religious, or
racial reasons — and a man could be blackballed for any
of these — did not get in. I accepted the exclusionary conditions without hesitation; I was in and that was what
counted most. The fraternity did give me a chance to
lead. I was elected president of the house. Buoyed by this
success, I ran for president of the student council and lost.
I ran for vice president and won. In the spring of my junior year I was one of twelve men chosen to be members
of the senior honors society.

The experience on the student council was blemished
by a decision I made to take over a project organized by a
graduating friend. The project was a student discount
card that entitled students to lower prices from merchants
who were eager enough for the business to pay to have
their names on the cards. The cost of the cards was a few
hundred dollars less than the revenue from the merchants. I got approval of the project from the council
without disclosing that I was earning money, which I presumed, was obvious. The presumption led to a call for
an investigation, which concluded I had done nothing
wrong. But my integrity had been called into question because I had not been careful about the appearance of a
conflict.

I decided not to approach the council with a problem
created by the only failing grade I earned in college in a
semester course in the Air Force Reserve Officers' Train-

ing Corps. The instructor judged me to be incorrigible and undisciplined during close-order drill and inspections. Because the university required all men to complete four semesters of ROTC in order to graduate, I needed to either get the rule changed or alter my behavior. I chose the first option, and led a grassroots campaign to persuade the university chancellor to change the policy. In my fourth year the university made the courses optional.

Before I could qualify for a pharmacist's license, I had to work for a year as an intern under the supervision of a licensed pharmacist. One of my best friends in the fraternity lived in Rushville, a town of twelve hundred in the heart of Nebraska's sand hills, three hundred miles north and west of Lincoln. His father was publisher of a weekly newspaper. They knew the local pharmacist who was looking for a low-cost employee. I took the job and lived with my friend's family.

Rushville is a dusty town, and if you approach from the east or west on U.S. Highway 20 when the grass is high and green it looks like a raft at sea. Driving northwest on a steady wind, you can be tricked into seeing the hills move like rolling waves. Looking north of Rushville a ridge of pine trees marks the beginning of a large Lakota Sioux reservation across the Niobrara River and the border into South Dakota. In all other directions hills of grass roll as far as the eye can see. At night when the sky is clear and the stars are bright, you can drive a car along the back roads without headlights. And if you lie on the ground and stare up at those stars, everything suddenly seems possible as if you are possessed by magic.

The writer Mari Sandoz grew up near Rushville. She wrote *Old Jules*, the story of her Swiss immigrant father, and *Cheyenne Autumn*, the story of Red Cloud, the last Sioux rebellion and pursuit by the U.S. Army. I read both that summer and had my view of the west transformed.

Sandoz describes the two great conflicts of the west. The first was the conflict between the settlers and the natives, whose attitudes toward the land were incompatible. The settler needed title to his property. The Native Americans were still hunter-gatherers and could not survive in a world where land was subdivided and sold to private owners. The second conflict was between the rancher who wanted grazing land and the farmer who brought the plow to break and turn the sod. Disease and force resolved the first conflict with the Native Americans in favor of the settler. Though there was violence between the rancher and farmer, it was drought that gave victory to the rancher.

The settlers who survived this country were not timid souls. They risked their lives in the pursuit of their dreams, and they never knew what lay ahead of them. Some knowledge guided their choices, but it was mostly the instinct for living free and unencumbered that drove them. Of course a prairie blizzard can change a snug little sod house into a frozen cell and make a person—often a young wife left alone while her husband made a long trip to the closest town—so lonely and dejected that death was preferable to life.

So I learned early that romantic dreams of the west are best left in the movie house. *Old Jules* typified the extremes of the western personality in a single man who was brave and determined with an explorer's spirit. And that same man hated the idea of his daughter becoming a writer. He called writers "the maggots of society" in part because he regarded any activity that did not produce something practical to be a drain on the energies of those who did the real work.

On my first weekend in Rushville, I went to a fundraiser at the American Legion Club sponsored by the Catholic Church. The party featured gambling, whiskey, and Rocky Mountain oysters, a delicacy made of thinly sliced beef or sheep testicles. That evening I met two sisters from Hays Springs, a town ten miles west on Highway 20. One was my age and the other two years younger. My second weekend they invited me to go swimming at Smith Lake. We stayed at the lake until the sun set and the stars came out. My imagination had not prepared me for this moment. Suddenly the world had become a much larger and more exciting place.

The world of voting in real elections was opened to me during college. In 1964 I reached twenty-one and cast my first vote in that year's election. My host family in Rushville heavily influenced the choices of political party and candidate. The father believed in limited government, which meant he usually lined up with Republican views rather than Democratic. I heard those views every Thursday night after he had finished printing and distributing his weekly paper.

On Thursdays he came home stained with ink and lead type. He engaged us in a lively discussion of history and politics. He was well read, strongly opinionated, and understood the lessons of history better than any person I had heard until then. He preferred freedom to government interference, advocated risk instead of guarantees of security, and preached the gospel of solving your own problems rather than complaining that life had treated you unfairly.

When I returned to classes in September 1963, I felt more aware of the importance of national politics thanks to these Thursday night discussions. But nothing that year affected me more than November 22, 1963, when Lee Harvey Oswald assassinated President John Kennedy. I was in the university library when I heard the news and quickly walked down R Street to my fraternity house to watch television. I stood in the card room of our house with other men who could not believe what they were seeing. I had not known such events were possible. They happened only in history books. Now the violence described in these books was visiting our lives.

Heavily influenced by my Rushville experience, I registered as a Republican. In November 1964 I cast my vote for Barry Goldwater, the man who was described as too extreme and bloodthirsty to be trusted with the nuclear button. My first vote was for a losing cause. Johnson's landslide victory included a Democratic win in Nebraska, a nearly unheard of event. I was told that if I voted for Barry Goldwater America would get deeper into the Vietnam War. Well, that is exactly what happened.

In the summer of 1964 as the presidential campaign was heading into its convention stage, I was taking a course in physics at Creighton University in Omaha. I had rented an apartment and found part-time work. President Johnson did not appear to be in any real trouble, but he was still concerned that Goldwater was scoring political points by accusing him of being weak on Communist aggression against South Vietnam. The president was looking for a chance to display his toughness. In the first week of August, two American destroyers were attacked in North Vietnam's Gulf of Tonkin, giving Johnson what he needed. He went to Congress and requested enactment of a resolution authorizing him to use whatever force was needed to respond to this aggression. On August 7, as my family was celebrating my mother's fiftieth birthday, both houses of Congress passed the authorization. With the passage of this resolution, life as I knew it was over. I did not know it at the time but within a year I would.

Black Elk, a famous Lakota Sioux medicine man, told the poet John Neihardt: "It is in the darkness of their eyes that men get lost." This darkness is a blind spot that prevents us from seeing that which we need to know most of all. The darkness makes it more difficult for us to tell right from wrong. We sleepwalk and respond to commands we do not challenge. We are guided by blind habit. When I left college in the spring of 1965, I was very much the sleepwalker. Looking back, the darkness in my eyes covered a very large territory.

10

MY FIRST JOB OUT OF college was in Onawa, Iowa, a town of three thousand on the eastern side of the high-water bank of the Missouri River. I worked in one of the town's two pharmacies. Before I could take the licensing examination, I needed six more months of practical experience and six more credit hours acceptable to the university. My job took care of the first. A correspondence course and a class at Morningside College in Sioux City, an hour's drive north of Onawa, took care of the second.

My salary at the pharmacy was one thousand dollars a month, enough to buy my first brand-new car and rent an apartment. I lived upstairs in a two-story white frame house with an open porch on two sides of the first floor and a screened-in sleeping porch on the second. Downstairs was a small nursing home that provided care for six.

On my first night I was awakened by a phone call from a man who worked downstairs. "There's something wrong with one of the patients. Can you come look at her?" I pulled on a pair of jeans and went down. A heavyset man about my age was waiting on the front porch. He took me back to a bedroom where an old woman lay on a bed. She had been dead a while. Her skin was cold to the touch, and her eyes were open and lifeless. She wore glasses and a Bible lay on the floor, apparently the last thing she read. A rosary was on the nightstand along with a bracelet and wedding ring. I thought I saw a look of surprise on her face. Though I had received no training in emergency services, the people of Onawa would have been surprised if the pharmacist had declined to be of assistance. So I confirmed the death and the young man called the funeral home.

I finished a five-year pharmacy program in four years but was three credit hours short of what I needed for graduation. The closest college was in Sioux City, Iowa, a Missouri River town fifty miles northwest of Onawa.

In order to get to work when the store opened at 10 A.M., I enrolled in the only class at Morningside College that began at 8 A.M. The class was on the New Testament. My first week the professor talked about U.S. involvement in a war between North and South Vietnam. He said we were dropping lots of bombs hoping to gain a quick victory. He told us the operation was called Rolling Thunder. Though he had served in and supported our military, he thought President Johnson was wrong to escalate the war and that Congress was wrong to have passed the Gulf of Tonkin Resolution. He spoke to us in clear, passionate terms, but neither his clarity nor his passion awakened me to the possibility I might end up in Vietnam. I assumed I would have to serve but likewise assumed I could avoid this war.

Since President Johnson's landslide victory in 1964, the scene in Vietnam had changed considerably. In February 1965, in retaliation for an assault on U.S. advisers in South Vietnam, Johnson had ordered a bombing attack against North Vietnam that he said would continue in support of our ally, South Vietnam. In March, U.S. Marines landed near Da Nang. In April a North Vietnam MIG—the fighter plane supplied by the Soviet Union— shot down a U.S. plane. In May an antiwar "teach-in" that was broadcast to more than one hundred U.S. campuses did not keep Congress from voting on June 8 to authorize the use of ground troops in direct combat if the government of South Vietnam requested it.

By July, 125,000 U.S. troops were in Vietnam, and the president announced a doubling of the draft call. McGeorge Bundy, Special Assistant for National Security Affairs, expressed supreme confidence when he said, "The

Vietcong are going to collapse within weeks. Not months, but weeks." And as the draft calls went out the protests escalated.

In 1965 those protests were dwarfed by the civil rights demonstrations for passage of the Voting Rights Act. In February, Malcolm X was shot in Harlem. In March a voter registration march in Selma, Alabama, turned ugly as Alabama State police used tear gas, whips, nightsticks, and dogs to turn back demonstrators as they walked on the highway to Montgomery. On the street, discontent was running ahead of political will. In spite of the Voting Rights Act becoming law on August 6, five days later riots broke out in the Watts area of South Central Los Angeles. Over a period of six days, thirty-four people were killed, most of them black. A symbol of how fear and ignorance had driven white and black America apart was that the airing of *Amos and Andy* was suspended until after the Watts riots. Until then it had been a popular show for white audiences.

As President Johnson continued to increase the number of men sent to Vietnam, the gap widened between the number of volunteers and the number needed by our armed services. Thus the number of men who had to be conscripted increased, particularly for the army and the Marine Corps. Suddenly my draft status was becoming an issue. I had registered with my local selective service board when I turned eighteen. When I enrolled in college, I was given a student deferment. Now that I was no longer a college student, I was eligible for service pending a physical and mental examination. If a letter arrived telling me to report for a physical, military service would not be far behind.

I could have avoided being drafted by claiming a physical disability because of my asthma. By then my medical file had fifteen years of diagnoses and treatments. I cannot imagine I would have had much difficulty getting letters from my doctors saying I was unfit for the military. But I never considered this an option. If Coach Bauer found me fit enough for football, I was fit enough for the U.S. armed forces. My youthful competitive urge had not changed.

But the reading for my New Testament class was bringing about a change. A transformation of my spirit seemed to occur late one summer night in Onawa as I sat in a wicker rocking chair on the screened porch of my apartment reading a book by Rudolph Bultmann. A cool breeze blew and the hum of the cicadas and the smell of cut grass calmed me and helped focus my attention on the words in the book. A hundred-watt lightbulb lit the pages. We were assigned a chapter, but I read the book from cover to cover.

Bultmann argued that the myths used by the first-century writers of scriptures needed to be demythologized and remythologized to be understood today. He had examined original documents and believed the language of the scriptures had to be understood in the context of what was being said and done in the first century A.D. Bultmann had been a chaplain to German soldiers in the Great War like his contemporary, Paul Tillich. Tillich was also on our recommended reading list, and as I watched the sunrise turn the dark front lawn into a field of green and yellow, I decided to read him next. My stomach growled with hunger, but I felt another hunger that morning, a calling that would require a change in my life's course.

I phoned my father for his advice. I told him I was thinking about changing careers. Over the line I could hear his confusion. "What did you have in mind?" he wanted to know. "I was thinking about religion," I said. "I read a book last night that really moved me. It made me wonder if I was doing the right thing." He advised me to finish what I had started, sounding as if I had made him uncomfortable.

Over the Labor Day weekend I changed jobs. I found a position at a large pharmacy in Sioux City that paid five hundred dollars more a month than I was making in Onawa. I rented a house on the south bank of the Missouri River and continued my religious readings. And I read a book for pleasure that fall: Herman Wouk's *The Caine Mutiny*.

Just after Halloween I received a letter from the draft board directing me to report the following Saturday to an address in downtown Omaha. I drove the slow route across the Missouri and then south on Highway 75 along the river through a half-dozen small sleeping communities. The road winds through hilly country that has frustrated many a farmer trying with little success to get a row crop to hold in the eroding soil. I watched the sun rise fast and red through cottonwoods and scrub oak.

Downtown Omaha was empty on that cold morning. At the draft office, a dozen men stood outside smoking on the sidewalk. I parked and joined them. The office was not yet open, so I walked up the street to an old building with a clock tower on its east side. Notices pasted on the windows warned trespassers to keep away.

Ignoring the warnings I climbed the red marble stairs and passed through an arched portal into a dark, abandoned entrance. Sixty years of accumulated soot from car exhaust and the coal-fired engines of the Union Pacific locomotives had darkened the red sandstone and pink granite. The windows in the heavy doors were caked with dirt. I rubbed my leather-gloved fist on the glass until I made a circle large enough for me to look in. Light streamed down from above into a space that could have been a church. I saw human figures in the mosaic floor but could not distinguish more. From my construction days I knew that the men who had worked on the project must have felt more pride in this accomplishment than in anything else they had done in their lives.

A flyer pasted on the door told of a small group of preservationists who were trying to save the old building. There was a plan to demolish it and erect a Hilton hotel.

It was part of an effort to attract conventions and help re-
vitalize a deteriorating downtown. The plan went ahead.
In May the heavy equipment came and tore the old post
office down.

I arrived back at the draft office just as a man in an
army uniform was ordering us upstairs into a classroom.
We found chairs and were handed multiple-choice tests
and told to complete them in silence with our number
two Ticonderoga pencils. After the test we were told to
move our chairs aside and prepare for our physical exam.
Preparation meant to strip down to your underwear. One
by one a doctor examined our puny chests with a cold
stethoscope, prodded our abdomens, and directed us to
turn our heads and cough.

I was told I would be notified of my status and should
expect a draft notice very soon thereafter. Now I had a decision to make: wait for the army to draft me or volunteer
for one of the other services. I took the faster interstate
back to Sioux City. On the way I decided I would not wait
for the army. I would apply for the navy. Herman Wouk's
tale of the sea was the decisive factor.

The following week I asked my employer for a day off
to visit the navy recruiter in Omaha. He advised me to
apply for Officer Candidate School (OCS), but because
it would take some time to get an answer, he suggested
that I go back to college for long enough to restore my deferment and then join the Fleet Reserve. I called the dean
of the pharmacy college in Lincoln to explain the situa-

tion, and he invited me to return to do research. I asked if he could suggest a subject. He told me of a team investigating the effects of digitalis on the heart tissue of rabbits. It sounded good to me, and for the next four months a hundred or more rabbits laid down their lives so I could become an officer in the world's largest and most powerful navy. My acceptance notice arrived in the spring. In October 1966 I entered the Fleet Reserve of the United States Navy. I was now a seaman recruit.

The writer and scientist Loren Eiseley's story about a catfish is a perfect metaphor for how my choice now appears to me. Eiseley liked to explore the Platte River in all seasons, and one winter as he was walking along the banks between Lincoln and Omaha he came upon a smooth, clear piece of ice and was startled to see a live whiskered catfish staring back up at him. Apparently the fish remained in the shallows too long one night and the water changed form.

Eiseley chopped an ice block around the fish, hauled it back to his car, and put it in a bucket he had in his trunk. He drove home and put the bucket in his basement planning to transfer the fish to a tank and keep him there until the spring thaw. Then Eiseley would return the catfish to the Platte. Days later he went downstairs and discovered the catfish dead on the concrete floor. When the ice thawed the catfish gambled that one good jump would take him from the prison of the bucket to the freedom of the river. He lost his bet.

11

ONE AFTERNOON IN February 1967, the day I was to report for the flight to Newport, Rhode Island, where I would begin Officer Candidate School, I packed the clothes on the list supplied by the navy and said good-bye to my mother and father. A college friend who was driving me to Omaha for my flight east picked me up in his red Chevrolet Corvette and drove to a downtown Lincoln bar, where three or four other friends met us.

The place had shuffleboard and a pool table. We drank beer, played pool, and listened to the jukebox. Someone kept playing the closest thing to a modern martial tune, Nancy Sinatra's "These Boots Are Made for

Walkin'." As the clock approached my departure time we began to sing the lyrics.

> These boots are made for walkin' and that's just
>   what they'll do,
> And one of these days these boots are gonna walk
>   all over you.

When it was time to go the moment did not seem special. The air was not charged with suspense. We didn't shake hands or embrace; a few slaps on the back, and I was out the door. With a clear sky and warm temperatures we put the top down for the ride to Omaha. On the way my friend's car ran out of gas. A stranger in a station wagon saved me from being absent without leave on my first day of active duty.

I arrived in Providence, Rhode Island, in the early evening and rode a steel-gray navy bus to Newport with ten or fifteen others. We checked into the Viking Hotel and I went to bed without stopping in the bar where I suspected there would be a gathering of other candidates. I woke in the morning to find the bus out front. I could tell from the size of the waiting crowd that there would not be an empty seat for the short trip to the base.

We passed through the gates of the school and pulled to a stop in front of a building named Nimitz. I dismounted warily and was ordered by a stern-sounding officer into a formation of three columns. We were given our first "forward march" and in ragged fashion proceeded to one building where our heads were shaved, another where clothing and bedding were stacked in our outstretched arms, and a third where we were assigned a room and a roommate. By coincidence and good fortune my roommate was a classmate and fraternity brother of mine at the University of Nebraska.

Although the men in our class were from many backgrounds, professions, and places in the United States, our shaved heads and identical uniforms made us remarkably alike. That, of course, is the idea in the military. Reducing free will and choice, and increasing uniformity and standardization makes it easier to create a team that works and fights as one. In many ways medals go against the spirit of the military and are in conflict with the goal of serving a higher purpose.

The weather in Newport was cold and stormy. The winds blowing off Narragansett Bay were worse than any snowstorm on the plains. Freezing water blew through my heavy peacoat, wool shirt, and long underwear. I wished Herman Wouk had included an explicit warning of this hazard in his novel. After we marched half a mile in the freezing gale to lower the American flag for the night, the sight of Old Glory for me would forevermore produce the recollection of a chill.

Each day we trained from 5 A.M. until lights out at 10 P.M. In eighteen weeks we had to learn enough of the fundamental skills of being a reserve naval officer to earn the respect of the regular officers who had spent four years at the academy or in ROTC programs. We studied essential subjects like navigation, semaphore, and damage control, but other assignments seemed more like harassment. We had to get the floor of a bathroom — or *head* as it is known in the navy — clean enough to eat off or spit shine our dress shoes till they reflected our faces. We had to learn how to render a salute, where to pin the brass military insignia, the fundamentals of marching in formation, and much other military protocol.

My earlier problems with military discipline did not vanish. In my second month I wrote a letter directly to our commanding officer protesting a change of policy. When I had enlisted I was told that if I failed to pass officer's training, I would be sent out to the fleet as an enlisted man. Now I was being told I would be discharged, reclassified 1-A, and drafted by the army.

My letter to the commanding officer of the school was naïve and arrogant. I said I was "irritated" with this "casual reversal." I argued that "when I took my oath I pledged solemnly to give life if need be in service. But they're quite willing to break the contract for reasons that seem far more petty than those that prompted us to volunteer." The commanding officer did not answer my letter. He told my company commander, who hit the ceiling. He told me I had violated proper procedures by not discussing it with him first, and I lost liberty privileges for two weekends. Nevertheless, the policy was changed, and I was promoted to assistant company commander.

The key differences between life in the military and life as a civilian are that in the military one must follow orders, respect the chain of command, and understand the nature of command. The essence of being a civilian in the United States is learning how to do the opposite, such as making free and independent choices and answering simple questions. What am I going to do this morning? What clothes will I wear? Where do I want to live? Who do I want as my friends? It is certainly true that a long list of external factors reduces our freedoms, but not like they do in the military.

In the military freedom is surrendered the moment the oath of loyalty is administered. Harsh rules enforced by a range of penalties and less due process minimize freedom. The most significant difference between the military and civilian worlds, and the most important thing I learned in eighteen weeks of officer training, was what it means to be in command, or as it is described in the navy, to "have command" or "the con."

In *The Caine Mutiny*, the men knew they could not refuse to follow orders simply because they didn't like their captain. The fact that he was strange or obsessive about strawberries was not cause for their actions. They had to prove their captain was no longer capable of command — and the burden of proof was high and difficult to achieve — or they would be committing the crime of mutiny, the penalty for which can be death.

When a military man or woman assumes responsibility

for commanding others, rule number one is this: you can delegate your authority to others in your command to perform duties you assign them, but you cannot delegate the responsibility for what happens while you have command. In civilian life excuses and lawsuits follow failure, and the game often seems to be to blame everyone but the person in charge. Civilians often think the military way is extremely unfair and harsh. It doesn't seem right to mete out severe punishment to someone who only missed a small detail.

One of the smallest and best examples of this difference is a rule that every man or woman learns who has worn the uniform of the United States of America: Failure to get the word is no excuse. In civilian life the most common and effective excuse for failure is "no one told me." In civilian life the burden shifts and the culprit will point his finger at someone else who should have told him when and where to report and how much gear to bring. In the military the burden does not shift. If debarkation time is 0700 and you show up at 0715 rubbing sleep out of your eyes saying that you didn't get the word, you will be punished. Again, it seems harsh, but the military simply could not function as a fighting force if it went by civilian rules.

Most serious of all is the burden on a commanding officer if his ship or unit fails in its mission. Then — even if he has no direct hand in the failure — he is responsible. If his ship or unit succeeds he gets credit for the success. This is the military way, and it cannot be otherwise. The

downside of this standard is the tendency for career officers and enlisted men to avoid risk, knowing the seriousness of the penalty for failure. The upside is that everyone
learns to pay attention to the smallest detail, which could
be the very thing that brings the entire operation down.
That detail may result in either a medal of commendation
or a court-martial.

We also learned how the bureaucracy of the navy
functioned. It did not take long to figure out that the
organization with the most power over your life was the
Bureau of Personnel, BUPERS. BUPERS issued your orders, and your orders told you where and when to report
for duty if and when you became a naval officer. You
would be allowed to express your preferences for duty, but
the needs of the navy would always take precedence.

In March I listened to a presentation about a possibility I had not considered when I enlisted. I heard a naval
officer tell us why we should think about applying for
underwater demolition training or UDT School. He said
it was the toughest training in all the military services. Its
graduates were known as frogmen, and they had a brave
and distinguished legacy. Frogmen were created during
the Second World War when their skills at beach reconnaissance and explosives saved the lives of many who
made amphibious assaults. UDT School would teach
scuba, demolitions, and the techniques of clandestine operations. He warned us that fewer than twenty-five percent of those who began UDT School would finish, and

that we would need mental toughness more than physical strength to survive.

The most important test of OCS — especially for land-locked men like me — came in mid-April when we were given the chance to command a seagoing vessel. It was an eighty-five-foot, twin-screw, steel-hulled boat big enough to replicate what we would experience in the real navy. In navigation class we had studied the details of Narragansett Bay and knew the depths and channels as they appeared on the charts. We had studied the rules at sea, knew how to avoid colliding with approaching ships by calculating their speed and distance, and other essential skills. But all this was theory; in practice, I did not know if I could command my own ship.

When the moment arrived I wondered if I would forget everything I had been taught. On the bridge I ordered the crew to cast off the bow and stern lines in preparation for embarkation. I ordered power first to the starboard and then port screws to maneuver the boat away from the pier. Underway I slowly increased speed as we passed the few boats that were in the water this early in spring. It wasn't a pretty departure, and I took longer than a more experienced hand but I had succeeded.

I negotiated the channel and was soon heading out into open water. I could feel the bow of the ship as it cut through the waves and the power of the engines ready to take me where I directed them to go. The eastern horizon of the Atlantic was dark and foreboding. The ocean beckoned to be explored as if I were the first to be on her back. The rocking motion and the salty air were intoxicating. The anticipation of failure had been the same as I felt when I first went on the football practice field. However, unlike football, the sensation of command at sea was more exhilarating than I had imagined it would be when I read Wouk's *Caine*. When we pulled back into port and disembarked, I never felt more proud or confident in my life

Thus, it was a very difficult decision to choose to apply for underwater demolition training instead of accepting an assignment to the fleet as a junior officer. But UDT would still give me the chance to command smaller boats and to learn more rigorous skills. It seemed too exciting to pass up if I could get accepted. So, I applied, passed the physical, and was told by BUPERS I could report to the West Coast school in Coronado, California. It was a turning point with more dire consequences than I imagined.

My roommate from Nebraska had also decided to take the examination and had also been given the chance to sign up for UDT. We both said yes, but the navy had other ideas for him. Somehow Admiral Hyman Rickover, father of the nuclear submarine program, had discovered that my roommate had graduated with high honors from engineering school. That led to an interview in the admiral's Washington, D.C., office, which led him away from UDT into subs. I would be going to Coronado on my own.

In May as the glory of spring arrived in Newport and

just before I was awarded my ensign bars, I went to the Jazz Festival along with many soon-to-be junior naval officers. The music was fabulous and the crowd young and enthusiastic. I felt right at home. Wandering about in my naval uniform I was hoping to meet the love of my life. Then Joan Baez spoke of her opposition to the war in Vietnam. She urged the men in the audience to say no to the war and gave this advice to the women, "Say yes to the boys who say no."

The audience cheered wildly. Afterward I thought I saw a changed look on the faces of people I passed. I imagined I saw anger, disrespect, and disgust. But that night after the concert I was very happy to discover that the women at the bar in the Viking Hotel were not following Joan Baez's advice.

I could not fail to notice that popular sentiment was beginning to turn against the war. The civil rights leader and Nobel laureate Martin Luther King had spoken out in opposition. In March there had been protests after the United States rejected Ho Chi Minh's offer to begin peace talks if bombing was halted and all U.S. troops were withdrawn. Rather than pulling back, we had escalated our effort. The number of men being sent to Vietnam grew daily, and reports of enemy setbacks became more frequent. As the war grew, so did the protests. In April a demonstration in New York attracted over one hundred thousand people, the largest crowd to date.

But I wasn't going to New York; I was going to Nebraska where antiwar protests were unlikely and then on to Coronado where they were nonexistent. I was no longer the graduate pharmacist I had been a year earlier. I was now a United States naval officer and felt a sense of serving something large and good: our nation's defense, the protection of home, tradition, history, stories of bravery and glory. I felt a part of it all.

After ten days' leave I flew to San Diego and caught the ferry that was the fastest way across the bay to Coronado Island. The smell of salty air and the bright, warm sun greeted me like a long-lost friend. The ferry carried me south across the harbor's narrow neck. To the west was the Pacific Ocean and east was Coronado Bay. I recognized the silhouettes of ships I had memorized at OCS: aircraft carriers, cruisers, destroyers, destroyer escorts, transport ships, landing craft, and mine sweepers.

Coronado felt like Lincoln with an ocean, sand, palm trees, and sunshine 365 days a year. On the island were two navy installations: an air station and the amphibious base that would be my home for the next two years. I was assigned an apartment on the second floor of the officers' quarters. From my balcony I looked west across a strand of beach that ran from San Diego in the north to Imperial Beach and Tijuana, Mexico, in the south and separated Coronado Bay from the Pacific Ocean. I dumped my gear, ate a quick meal at the officers club, and returned to the balcony where I watched my first sunset over the ocean. I thought the navy had sent me to paradise.

The base was a collection of single-story office buildings for two commands: the boat command that operated
the vessels used for amphibious assaults and the training
command for UDT. To support these commands, there
were maintenance shops, personnel offices, classrooms, a
movie theater with a rounded roof, a small grocery store,
and separate dining facilities for officers and enlisted
men. Across the highway on the strand of beach were
the long, low buildings where men were sent when they
had finished training and joined UDT Eleven, Twelve, or
Thirteen.

In the morning I reported for duty to the Naval Special
Warfare Group, Pacific, where I learned that UDT class
did not begin until the first week of September. Over the
next fourteen weeks I crammed in a two-week class in amphibious tactics, a two-day pistol course that was supposed
to produce expert marksmen but achieved far less in my
case, and a two-day rifle course that yielded the same result. I ran on the beach and swam in the ocean every
morning and in the evening explored the nightlife of San
Diego. I found an ad for a four-year-old red Volkswagen
bus that I bought for a few hundred dollars. With this I
widened my circle of exploration east and north into the
coastal mountains and across into the Sonoran Desert.

In *War and Peace*, Leo Tolstoy, who served with the
Cossacks, observed that we human beings struggle with
the idea of leisure time because it makes us feel guilty
when we are doing "nothing." But, he said, there is one

place where enforced idleness is institutionalized: the military. There, he said, you are expected to spend your time doing nothing. That certainly described my existence in the summer of 1967.

My hardest task in the morning after a run, a swim, and breakfast was reading the *San Diego Union*, trying to understand what was going on in the world. In June I read about the Six Day War in Israel, China's detonation of a hydrogen bomb, and race riots across the country that killed seventy-seven people in 125 cities. After this exertion I would drive to some place I wanted to see: Los Angeles, San Francisco, Tijuana, the mountains, the desert, or the ocean. Even when classes were being held I had large blocks of time for standing around and contemplating life or listening to others complain about some trivial inconvenience.

As the summer wound down I was given an unexpected gift: the approach of Labor Day without asthma symptoms. Apparently the absence of the prairie grasses was all I needed to breathe normally. My UDT classes began on the Friday afternoon after my twenty-fourth birthday. We were issued a pair of black leather combat boots, three pairs of green fatigue pants with matching shirts, one soft green hat, one hard fiber helmet liner, two pairs of khaki swimming trunks, one pair of coral booties, one snorkel, and one face mask. After we got our gear we were told to form columns of seven on the street between the UDT offices and the bay.

The senior officer in our class stood in front of a formation of about twenty-five columns, each headed by an
officer with six enlisted men behind him. We waited at
parade rest until a dark-skinned chief petty officer with
what looked like coral poisoning on his legs walked out
from behind the training offices. He wore the frogman
uniform of khaki shorts with a blue and gold T-shirt. He
swaggered over to the senior officer of our class and,
rather than giving a smart salute, he lowered his head to
the right and drew his right hand up lazily as if to say, You
have not yet earned my full respect. Then he spat a stream
of tobacco juice on the ground close to the officer's shoes.

"My name is Olivera," he said, "and you are the sorri-
est group of bananas I have ever seen." He then proceeded to give us a simple set of instructions. We could
quit anytime we wanted, now or later. We simply had to
go to the back of the training compound, rap our helmet
on the door, and shout the two words, "I qweeet." He said
he hoped and expected that more than half of us would
say those magic words before we completed the course.
He said our most important command was "Drop!" When
we heard this command we were to drop to the ground
and start doing push-ups. We could not stop or stand up
until we heard the command, "Recover!" And when we
recovered we were to shout, "Hoo Yah!" followed by the
name of the person who had ordered us to drop.

Each seven-man column became a boat crew that was
expected to carry or paddle a small inflatable rubber boat

(IBS) everywhere we went for the next eighteen weeks. Our training would begin on this same street at 6 A.M. Monday. Olivera told us to be there in formation with our boots spit-shined, our uniforms starched, our insignia sewn on our collars or shirtsleeves, and our names stenciled in black over our left shirt pockets. When our senior officer protested that this would be impossible because the laundry services were closed, Olivera took a step closer, spit on the ground, and said, "I expect you bananas to be standing tall at 0600 with everything done as I have asked. That means every one of you. If even one man is not ready, I'll march all of you into the bay. Dismissed."

Over the weekend we found a way to do what he told us. In my first weekend I learned that one of the sacrosanct boundaries I had learned in Newport — that it was taboo for officers and enlisted men to fraternize — was not sacrosanct in the teams. We still respected the chain of command. Enlisted men called us "sir," and we called them by their last names. Those in command were still held accountable, but in practice we worked as a team. We simply depended on each other too much for officers and enlisted men not to become friends.

Other boundaries remained. There was one between the rest of the navy and us. We called them the "black shoe Navy" and they called us "squids." There was a boundary between those officers and enlisted men who did not expect to make the navy a career and the "lifers" who did, and one between reserve officers and regular officers, the reserve officers being lower in the social hierarchy.

All boundaries disappeared as we scrambled to do what Olivera had ordered us to do. We organized ourselves into teams. We found self-employed contractors who were willing to do the weekend of washing, ironing, printing, and sewing that we needed. Most important, we made certain that no man failed. Had each of us gone off on our own we most certainly would not have gotten the job done. Working together we managed with time to spare.

On Monday our shirts were stenciled with our names, our insignia were sewn in their proper places, our pants were hemmed, our entire uniforms including our hats were starched, and our boots were spit-shined and gleaming. We arrived early and stood tall in the dark waiting for Olivera to appear. We felt proud and were ready to begin. Olivera appeared on schedule. He gave our senior officer another half-hearted salute and inspected our ranks with a quick glance left and right. Then he told our senior officer to bring the men to attention, ordered them to execute an about-face and a forward march. Following these orders would put us into the cold, black water. Our senior officer objected, "But, Olivera, we did everything you told us to do." Olivera answered, "Mister, it's time for a little suffering. To succeed in this program you must be willing to die before you can go to heaven." We began our day soaking wet.

Our class was separated into two sections of about 120 each: alpha and bravo. At the beginning there were about twelve boat crews of one officer and six enlisted men. The sections trained together for the first six weeks, were separated for eight, and brought back together for the final four. Our daily schedule began with calisthenics on an open field near the training offices. Then we marched on the double across the highway to the beach, each boat crew carrying its IBS on its heads. Lowering our boats, we ran two miles to the chain-link fence at the air station past the Hotel del Coronado and the two miles back. We wore combat boots, and whether high tide or low, we were expected to finish in thirty minutes.

Those who could not keep up were selected by the instructors for the "goon squad" and were subjected to physical abuse, like having to do push-ups in the surf zone or run the course a second time. Knowing that life was going to get a lot more difficult was an incentive for the trainees to perform at the expected level. It was also an incentive for trainees to quit, which they began to do in our first week.

After the run we negotiated an obstacle course on the beach side of the base. This course also took a terrible toll on trainees, especially those who had been in the goon squad during the run. It was common for trainees to be run repeatedly through the course until their bodies gave them little choice but to hang it up and quit. Those who survived were marched on the double back across the highway to the pool. In the pool we swam with face masks and snorkels but without fins. We were timed and daily increased our distance until we were circling the pool for a mile.

During the first four weeks each boat crew learned how to handle its IBS as a team. The officer served as coxswain except on long distances, when most of us rotated with our enlisted men, not only to give them a break but also to increase the performance of the crew. We learned how to hold the wooden paddles to minimize noise and reflection. We learned how to navigate through heavy surf. We learned how to secure our gear. In short order, the IBS became a physical extension of our bodies and part of everything we did.

Week five was called Hell Week because we trained nonstop, with little or no sleep. Most casualties—men who simply could not go on—occurred before or during that week. Instructors paid closest attention to those men struggling with the threshold requirements: doing ten pull-ups at the beginning of calisthenics, completing the four-mile run in thirty minutes, finishing the obstacle course, and completing the swim in the allotted time. Other failures that could result in extra running, swimming, or push-ups included falling asleep in class, forgetting to attach some required piece of equipment to the IBS, or failing to say "Hoo yah!" when recovering from push-ups. Those men who didn't make it were certainly traumatized by the defeat. But stress can also bring out the best and that was what the instructors were looking for.

I will never forget one enlisted man in our class named Thompson who rose to the challenge with great dignity. He must have been forty pounds overweight. He failed all the threshold tests. He couldn't do ten pull-ups and was kept at the bar by shouting instructors who heaped insult upon insult on him. He was always in the goon squad during the run and was ordered to do head-stands in the surf zone, run wind sprints in shallow water, and do push-ups until all his strength was gone. On the obstacle course he could not pull himself over a twenty-foot wooden wall and was once kept there until dark while two instructors screamed themselves hoarse trying to get him to quit. In the pool his large legs and torso made keeping up impossible. He got better in swimming when we were issued swim fins in our sixth week. Thompson went from being one of the slowest swimmers to one of the fastest, but he continued to suffer on runs and the obstacle course.

Hell Week was a series of competitions between boat crews. Points were awarded for first, second, and third places. According to a rumor that our instructors would neither confirm nor deny, the winner of the week's competition would be excused from the week's final event: an all night ten-mile ocean race in our boats down the coast to Tijuana and back.

My boat crew was ahead on points at the end of the week. Even if we lost the next-to-last event before we set off on the ten-mile IBS trip, our lead was big enough to win. That event was a quarter-mile foot race from the calisthenics field to our boats. Before the race we were told to lie down on our backs and rest a few minutes without going to sleep. Anyone caught sleeping was ordered to jump in the bay and make the trip to Tijuana soaking wet. The event was held in the darkness after sunset, and after six sleepless days it was impossible to stay awake. Soon all of us had visited the water. At the starting line we were told this was to be a Le Mans racing start: each boat crew would run down to the finish line to launch its boat. The boats were in a row in front of the training headquarters.

At the sound of the whistle the run began. When we neared our boat, we saw an oval shadow lying on the ground. While the other crews were heading for water, we stood and stared at a sad and deflated boat. Worse, the hand pump, which was supposed to be attached to the gunnels, was missing. A missing pump meant lost points, which in turn meant we could not possibly win the grand prize. Olivera asked me what I intended to do. I said I would find the pump, repair the damage, and join the others who were now long gone. He spat once on the ground and said, "No, I think you bananas should secure for the night. You won that right."

We whooped and laughed for joy like children who had received the most special gift we could ever have imagined. I saluted and said, "Thank you, Olivera." We showered and went to our barracks to sleep and dream the dreams of champions.

The first five weeks of training reduced our ranks by a third. During week six we were issued swim fins and began learning how to do a beach reconnaissance from the ocean. We still did calisthenics and a run to start the day, but the amount of abuse we took dropped sharply. At the same time our respect for and knowledge of the ocean rose dramatically. We learned it was unpredictable and more dangerous than it looked. A cold stream, the Japanese current, dropped water temperatures to the high fifties as early as October. Even in our wet suits an hour of exposure produced some very chilled young men. Often a man could not walk when he emerged from the icy water after a thousand-meter beach reconnaissance.

After week six I spent four weeks on scuba and four weeks on demolition. Scuba training in Coronado was a straightforward and deadly serious study of navy diving charts, the behavior of gases under pressure, and the mechanics of the device that regulates the flow of compressed air from a pair of ninety-cubic-foot tanks down a pair of rubber hoses into a mouthpiece. We divided our time between the classroom and the swimming pool, becoming familiar with the gear and our limits before we went to the ocean. Scuba would be more for recreation than for military operations, where we used swim fins, face masks, and snorkels.

On San Clemente Island, where goats, seals, and birds ruled, we learned how close death lurked. We were training to use plastic explosives, detonation cords, and fuse lighters to destroy both underwater and aboveground obstacles. We learned to tell a high- from a low-order explosion, how to calculate the size and shape of a charge needed to destroy various objects, and how to build our own explosives if government-issued materials were unavailable.

We were taught to organize our missions using the army's five-paragraph patrol order. This standard order helps the person in charge organize the operation and specify the mission's objective, describe in detail the terrain to be crossed, calculate the kind of gear needed, and determine the means of entry, the route to the objective, and the means of extraction and retreat. Communication call signs, fire support available, and other vital information are all part of a five-paragraph order.

One exercise entailed tying canvas satchels of plastic explosives to underwater concrete obstacles like those the Japanese had built in World War II. Our trainers thought these obstacles might be used again in some future conflict. A row of fifteen or twenty concrete pyramids topped with two protruding pipes was located just outside the surf zone. The obstacles were fifteen to twenty feet underwater, so the divers could see their target from the surface. Working in teams of two, the first swimmer in snorkel gear dove with the canvas bag of explosives, placed the strap of the bag over the pipes, and began fastening the bag to the concrete. When he could no longer hold his breath, he headed for the surface. The second swimmer started down when he saw his swim buddy coming up. After the bag was tied, an instructor dove down to inspect for mistakes. To complete this exercise satisfactorily, we had to tie off five obstacles.

During our first week on San Clemente, stormy seas churned the water and sand into a murky darkness. A swimmer at the surface could no longer see an obstacle on the bottom. To reduce the danger, the instructors' solution was to tie a plastic bottle to one end of a nylon line and the other end to the obstacle. A swim pair could find the obstacle by swimming out to the floating bottle and following the line down. The only problem was that the swimmer on the surface could not see the swimmer on the bottom.

We were two days behind schedule so our instructors had us working without a safety break at lunch. The safety break enables the instructors to check that all dive teams are accounted for. During the noon hour, dive teams only had time to grab a sandwich and run back to tie another obstacle. Just after lunch my swim partner and I were heading into the water when we heard a cry from the nearest swim pair, "There's someone floating on our line! It looks like Greco!" My partner, Baker, and I swam out to help. When we arrived Greco was floating just below the surface of the water with the nylon line wound around his right arm.

He had stayed at the bottom too long. Rising to the surface he probably had been rotating his arms, as is usual when ascending in water where visibility is poor. This caused the line to wrap round his right arm so that the line held him just short of the surface. He must have grabbed his swimming partner, McCoy, by the legs and pulled him down. He did not release him until both were unconscious. When death brought release, McCoy sank to the bottom. The plastic float gave Greco's body just enough buoyancy to keep it near the surface.

When Baker and I arrived, the other swim pair was frantically trying to untie Greco, thinking the line was still keeping him underwater. The opposite was the case. When we loosened the line, Greco's body sank like a rock and disappeared into darkness.

Baker, one of the strongest swimmers in the class, immediately dove for Greco. When he surfaced with the body he was gasping and sputtering with fear. "I swam right into his face. Look at his face. Look at it." Greco's face mask was still in place. His eyes were open and the glass was filled with green mucus.

We swam Greco's body to shore. One of the instructors tried to revive him with mouth to mouth but the exercise made him vomit and did nothing for Greco. He was long gone. He must have been on the line for at least half an hour. Then someone asked, "Where's McCoy?" An electronics technician who had recently been granted a substantial reenlistment bonus, McCoy was one of the smartest men in our class. Divers began searching for McCoy's body from a motorized Boston Whaler at the spot where Greco was found while we searched on shore. We hoped he had made the mistake of abandoning Greco. He would face a court-martial, but at least he would be alive. It was not to be. We heard a shout from the Whaler. "We've found him. We're bringing him up."

McCoy was dead. We gathered in a circle around the two bodies. The sky was gray and we shivered as the wind blew against our wet skin. The tragedy was a reminder of what could happen to any of us. The lead instructor then made the mistake of telling us to get back to work. I told him that we needed a break to absorb the deaths of our friends. The instructor yielded.

We returned to Coronado for the final four weeks of instruction. In this phase we learned advanced procedures for getting to our military destinations. One of these was exiting and entering a submerged moving submarine. Inside the sub we were told to climb up a steel ladder into a forward-locking chamber where we listened to the clanging of the hatch below being sealed, and a voice over a tinny-sounding loudspeaker told us what to do. We turned a valve to let the air escape, turned another to fill the chamber with water, and then turned the water valve off when it reached our chin. Twin ninety-cubic-foot scuba tanks were our source of air as the chamber filled. When the pressure of the water in the chamber equalized with the pressure outside, the hatch opened easily, allowing us to exit the submarine.

A more common method of dropping and picking up UDT swimmers was with a diesel-engine boat that had a top speed of twenty to twenty-five knots. An IBS would be lashed to the outside of the boat. The drop part was easiest. Swimmers would quickly enter the rubber boat single file and drop off the side with their fins, face mask, and snorkel. Pickup went in reverse. As the boat approached, the pickup man stood in the IBS holding out a ring-shaped hose to a line of swimmers. The swimmer would kick with his fins just before his arm hit the rubber ring, allowing the pickup man to pull him out of the water and into the IBS.

A considerable number of experiments were tried to improve the efficiency of drops and pickups. Efficiency and added risk were constantly at odds. A turboprop boat with a maximum speed of fifty knots delivered swimmers efficiently, but it could also knock a man unconscious. A metal cable attached to a helium-filled balloon, which was snagged by a fixed wing airplane, made for a terrific James Bond type of exit, but if the cable broke, the man picked up would exit life.

Rappelling is the most efficient and least risky means of descending from a helicopter onto land, or down the face of a building, or a steep natural incline. The rappel works by friction, in our case, the friction of a line against a metal link that slows the speed of fall.

In training we used two lines. A short line fastened around our thighs and waist formed a harness. The second and a longer line was the descent line. It was doubled for safety and anchored solidly at the point of departure.

An oval metal link was then snapped into the harness and attached to the descent line. A single turn of this line through the link was all that was needed to create the friction that became the difference between life and serious injury. To start the rappel we held the ascending part of the double line with our left hand and the descending part of the line with our right. We then looked over our left shoulder down to where we wanted to go. We could stop the rappel by bringing the descent line behind our backs. This was known as applying the brake. The brake could also be applied partially in order to slow the descent.

Safety took us first to the classroom, where an instructor demonstrated the physics of the rappel. Then we went into the obstacle course where we rappelled twenty feet into sawdust. Finally, we drove to a hydroelectric dam. There we anchored the double line to a steel handrail at the top of the 150-foot face. An instructor demonstrated the technique. He connected the line through the snap link, applied the brake with his right hand, and stepped over the handrail while facing the dam. Then he let go of the rail and jumped backward with his feet spread as wide

as his shoulders. The line tightened and he came grace-
fully to a stop, his legs braced on the concrete partway
down the dam. He repeated his descent several times, letting out more and more line each time. Finally he stood
at the bottom, unhooked the line from the link, and told
the first student to follow him.

A second instructor then helped the line of anxious
trainees hook up and jump. When my turn came I was
not the least bit afraid. I understood the science and had
seen it work with my own eyes. I was quite surprised when
I hooked up the line to the link, applied the brake, and
stepped over the handrail that my mind could not persuade my left hand to let go. I don't know how long I
would have stood motionless were it not for the instructor's sharp blow to my knuckles. Reflex did what thought
could not.

Letting go is never easy. We like to hold on to known
safety even when our minds are telling us to do otherwise.
This was a powerful lesson; another thing learned in the
navy I would apply all the days of my life.

By the end of training I was twenty pounds heavier
and felt more physically capable than at any time in my
life. I was ready for the teams. But during those eighteen
weeks my future had changed even more than my body
had. In November after we returned from San Clemente,
President Johnson made a trip to San Diego, and even
there he met war protesters. Some weeks before there had
been a 150,000-person demonstration at the Pentagon, re-

sulting in almost seven hundred arrests; it was so disturb-
ing to the Johnson Administration, the director of selective service announced that students arrested in antiwar
demonstrations would lose their draft deferments.

The protests did not stop President Johnson from
ramping up the U.S. commitment in Vietnam. The increased demand for troops changed the course of events
for those of us who completed UDT training after 1967.
Before the escalation we expected to be assigned to one of
three UDT teams in Coronado. But another option surfaced because of the war — direct recruitment into SEAL
Team One.

In the early 1960s President Kennedy, because of his
naval career in the Second World War, approved a navy
unit equivalent to the Army's Special Forces. The unit
would use the name SEAL, an acronym combining the
three methods of their insertion into combat areas: sea,
air, and land. The unit was formed of men from the underwater demolition teams and was kept largely secret
until a 1967 *Reader's Digest* article appeared called "War-
riors with Green Faces."

When our training was complete I was among twelve
asked to volunteer for SEAL Team One. I would be given
advanced training in the tactics of small units and would
likely attend both Army Airborne and Ranger Schools before being assigned to a SEAL Team One platoon headed
for Vietnam. Our instructors told us we could refuse the
assignment. If we did, we would not be assigned to one of

the UDT teams, but would be sent to a ship at sea, thus wasting all the training we had just endured.

On Monday morning the new "volunteers" gathered in a meeting room followed by a crowd of SEALs, all of us waiting for the arrival of the team's commanding officer, Captain Anderson. When he walked to the front we all came to attention. He told us to stand at ease and explained what SEAL Team One was and told us we had the right to refuse. All we had to do was stand to indicate that our answer was no. One man stood. It was Thompson, who had suffered more with good humor than any of us had in order to become a frogman. The instant he stood he was ushered from the room, and I never saw him again. His act was the bravest I had ever witnessed.

12

I HAD TWO WEEKS OF LIBERTY after graduating from training but did not make it home December 2 for my sister Jessie's wedding to Dean Rasmussen. By the time I got there, Nebraska was enjoying the coldest winter I had ever experienced. The marriage of my younger sister inspired me to spend several days and nights at my parents' lakeside cabin with a woman I had dated in college. We skated and sailed an iceboat until we were completely frozen and then sat by the fire talking about the possibility of a future together. The talks ended inconclusively.

In January I returned to Coronado and began my training for SEAL Team One with a six-week course on small arms and small unit tactics. After that I would take courses at the Army's Airborne and Ranger Schools at Fort

Benning, Georgia. I was in a new and different phase of my training. Before I had been taught how to blow things up. Now I was being taught how to kill. There was euphemism and other make-believe terminology to keep us from facing this truth, but occasionally that truth would appear in its full, unvarnished reality.

Vietnam was becoming a military and political quagmire. By the close of 1967, American casualties reached nearly a thousand a month. When the Communists launched the Tet Offensive on January 30, more than half a million American troops were on the ground in the country. The Tet battles, which lasted three weeks, resulted in forty thousand enemy deaths and were a decisive military victory for the South Vietnamese. But while the North and their Communist allies in the South failed on the battlefield, they succeeded with public opinion in the United States.

The aggressive ability of our enemy surprised many Americans who had supported the war. They were eloquently represented by Walter Cronkite, whose words "something is terribly wrong here" resonated throughout the United States. The constant assurances of our military and political leaders that we were winning the war did not square with the observations of those on the ground in Vietnam.

The Tet Offensive was still going on while I was in the SEAL team's six-week course. Our instructor was Chief Stone, a former sergeant in the army who had served in

Korea and joined the navy when he decided to return to military life. He was just what the navy thought their new special operations unit needed. To the navy he was a chief petty officer, but he looked and acted like he was still training soldiers in an infantry platoon. He organized the class by the book, teaching us such things as which foot to fire on when we advanced, how to execute small unit fire and maneuver, how to set an ambush with claymore mines, and how to avoid aiming an assault rifle high at night. We learned to assemble, disassemble, and fire the AR-15 or M-16 assault rifles and the M-60 automatic rifle. We practiced the M-79 grenade launcher, the light anti tank weapon or LAW, and the hand-thrown fragmentation grenade.

We learned to distinguish between the smaller .556 caliber rounds fired by the M-16 from the larger .762 NATO round fired by the M-60. We learned the difference between deadly "aimed fire" and firing a rifle for the effect of the noise. We were shown how to use nonstandard weapons like the carbine, the shotgun, the silenced 9-mm pistol, and the AK-47, a Soviet and Chinese assault rifle with a wooden stock that was popular with U.S. soldiers in Vietnam. We learned how to call in artillery and how to use Willy Peter rounds to mark the target. We learned basic first aid and began developing a list of standard operating procedures for Vietnam.

We practiced these procedures while patrolling and maneuvering in both day and night situations. Usually we operated in seven-man groups, learned to recognize hand signals so we could remain silent and eventually to read the person in front and behind us without intentional signals. We learned how to secure and inspect small buildings and why injured men could jeopardize the lives of an entire seven-man squad, since it took two men to carry one out, leaving too few to return fire during a withdrawal. We learned how and when to call in medevac helicopters and gunships, though we were told not to expect them always to be available. We practiced sitting for long periods of time without falling asleep and were warned to avoid amphetamines, since they often produced hallucinations. We learned how time and silence enabled us to notice what we had previously missed.

We learned more of the orienteering we had been taught in UDT. Orienteering is the technique of reading a topographical map, which uses grid lines to illustrate the varying elevations of the terrain. Each grid line represents a different elevation above sea level. A topographical map can be very confusing at first. But soon the curving lines begin to resemble hills, valleys, plateaus, gradual slopes, steep ravines, and other land formations. Navigating through unknown terrain becomes easier and you are less likely to get lost.

Under the right circumstances getting lost can be a good experience. Knowing that you are lost makes you humble and forces you to discover things about yourself. Out in the field it is the rare person who doesn't at least momentarily ask, "Where am I?" Sometimes the answer comes quickly. Sometimes not. Sometimes you are certain you know where you are only to discover miles and hours later that you were wrong. And sometimes you misread a land feature and get in trouble as a result.

That happened to me in an orienteering exercise during underwater demolition training. We were on a night compass course in the open hills and orchards that in 1967 were part of the San Diego landscape. The boat crews were competing. At about 3 A.M. our crew was ahead after three of the four legs. We knew the end of the leg was clearly marked by the trucks that would take us back to Coronado. We could not go wrong.

My crew and I avoided detection by reading our map under a plastic poncho with a red flashlight. Seven heads tried to interpret the curving lines that separated us from our goal. The most prominent feature on the map was a five-thousand-meter lake. We simply had to choose whether to walk down the left or the right side of the lake. The shorter distance was down the left side, but there the grid lines were stacked tight, right to the water's edge, meaning that the land was very steep, perhaps a sheer cliff. The right side of the lake was a much longer distance but the spacing of the grid lines was wide, indicating a level, easy walk. Most of the crew favored the safe bet, but I was convinced we would find a path on the left side that would take us quickly to the trucks.

Unfortunately we went with my instincts. Not only did

the cliff go right to the water's edge but the water was deep and cold. The best we could do was to make our way slowly along the face of the cliff. Every so often I would reassure my men with the words "there must be a path just a little ways farther; there must be a path." The sun was up and all the other crews were waiting for us in the trucks when we finally finished. And for years after, whenever I saw or talked to one of my crew, the phrase "there must be a path" was a guaranteed laugh line.

SEAL team orienteering was more realistic. We were training for military operations in terrain that resembled what we expected when we deployed. The place was east of the San Gabriel Mountains near the southern shore of the Salton Sea. The town closest to our camp was Niland, a community that existed to serve the needs of farmers in the Imperial Valley to the south. The irrigation canals were large enough to carry the river patrol boats that we would use in Vietnam.

At the end of the six weeks Lieutenant Arch Woodard, our senior officer, led us in the preparation of a critique of Chief Stone's course. We wrote a detailed description of improvements we thought were needed and put the report in a plastic folder along with an introductory letter to Chief Stone. We were granted a meeting. Chief Stone learned the reason for the meeting as we passed our report across his desk. In a single continuous motion and without breaking eye contact with us he threw our pages into a trash basket. Then he said in a friendly, respectful tone free of condescension, "That was an excellent report, Mr. Woodard. Was there anything else?" With that our meeting was over.

Our training was just beginning. In March I began Airborne and Ranger Schools at Fort Benning, Georgia. While I was there Minnesota Senator Eugene McCarthy, running against President Johnson as an antiwar candidate for the Democratic nomination for president, got forty-two percent of the vote in the New Hampshire primary. This surprise victory set the stage for president Johnson's remarkable and unexpected televised address on March 31. He announced that he would not be a candidate for a second full term in office. He promised to begin more serious negotiations with North Vietnam to end the war as quickly as possible. Though we did not know it at the time, this decision ended any hope that South Vietnam would survive as an independent country.

I was relieved that the war would be ending before I was ready to go. I thought that the reason for our involvement—the freedom and self-determination of the South Vietnamese—could not have been so important after all if we were willing to negotiate it away to North Vietnam. For this had to be the outcome of any negotiated settlement. Following their successful war with France, the Communists had yielded to Russian and Chinese pressure in Geneva to allow for the creation of two countries divided at the seventeenth parallel. They had begun a second war against South Vietnam in order to extend their political control over the entire Indochinese peninsula. In my mind the question of who would win this war was resolved on March 31, 1968. It was now only a question of time.

If President Johnson had faced the voters of Georgia in 1968 he probably would not have been forced out of the race. There are few places where the uniform of our military is more respected or where military personnel are made to feel so welcome. I came to know and love the red clay and pine tree–covered hills of Georgia better than any place I had ever been.

The objective of Airborne School is to train young men to do a very unnatural thing: to jump out the door of a perfectly good airplane. We would earn our jump wings after we successfully completed five static line jumps from a C-118 twin-engine aircraft using a T-10 parachute. The jumps were all in daylight, though we joked that it seemed like night, since so many of us closed our eyes as we stood in the door and jumped.

The basic physics of the parachute are simple: a fabric canopy fills with air and slows the descent of a falling object enough so that the object is not badly damaged when gravity brings it down to earth. Unlike most of today's civilian parachutists, we did not pull a rip cord to open the chute. That was accomplished by a static line attached to the parachute and connected by a snap link to another line that was anchored fore and aft to the bulkhead of the plane. When the plane approached the drop zone, a yellow light told the jump master to prepare his "stick" of jumpers by giving them two commands: "Stand up!" and "Hook up!" Then the door was opened and one by one we shuffled forward and waited for the jump master's command to jump.

We were supposed to jump out with both feet together in front of us, our hands to our sides, holding either end of our reserve parachute, and our heads tucked down. This position kept the body from tumbling when hit by the onrushing air. We were supposed to count, "One thousand, two thousand, three thousand," before looking up to see if our canopy had opened properly. If it had not, we were trained in emergency procedures that would deploy our reserve chute.

There was one contingency plan. When the main chute became entangled in the plane's tail, the runway was foamed and the plane would land. Just before we boarded for our first jump we were advised that the best position for survival in this situation was a tight tuck. Presumably, the function of the foam was to prevent spectators from witnessing the jumper's body being crushed on the runway's surface.

If the chute opened normally, as was the case nine times out of ten, then you had a minute or two to enjoy the ride. With a T-10 parachute the risk of getting hurt during the landing was quite high. Even if the wind was calm, the rapid descent could lead to trouble if you did not execute a proper parachute landing fall: feet tightly together, head tucked, and a safe roll in the direction of the fall. If the wind was blowing, the risk of injury rose; the only way to control the T-10's direction was to grab the two canvas risers that connected the harness to the canopy in the direction you wanted to go, and pull them to your chest. The maneuver—difficult to hold for very long—produced uncertain results.

As earth approached, we looked for smoke rising from flares that showed where we were supposed to land and the direction of the wind. Some of us tried steering our chutes by pulling two risers to slip toward the smoke. But this technique did not work with wind velocities over ten to fifteen knots, and with the metal helmets given jump school students in 1967, the chances of a serious head injury increased with the speed of the wind at ground level.

I managed to complete five successful jumps and received my wings in a closing ceremony that contained a brief but memorable military speech. The school's commanding officer said in a mock-serious tone that we were no longer the "sorry legs" that we had been before we earned our wings. "What are you?" he shouted. "Airborne!" we answered in one voice. "What are you?" he challenged again. "Airborne!"

The pride the group felt at that moment was palpable. I felt it, too. But not everything I saw at Airborne School made me feel proud. Airborne was supposed to be an elite program that accepted only the most highly qualified soldiers. My class contained a large number of poorly motivated, poorly trained soldiers, most of whom were also poor and black. Many of them did not complete the course and were sent, I suspected, to combat units in Vietnam. Afterward I would always believe that Vietnam was a poor man's war, no matter what was said to the contrary.

Twenty-four years later I returned to Georgia, as a candidate for the Democratic nomination for president. I spoke to students at Spelman College about what I had seen here in 1968. On stage with me was a small group of men and women who were supporting my candidacy, though it was clear that I could not possibly win. One of them was a black man about my age who introduced himself as one of my drill sergeants during Airborne School. He told me the large number of black soldiers I had seen were part of a program initiated by Secretary of Defense McNamara. The program authorized the army to lower its standards in order to meet its induction targets. This plan symbolized the tragic paradox of Lyndon Johnson's presidency. While fighting a war for civil rights and against poverty at home, he was sending minorities and the sons of poor families to die in Vietnam. On April 4, the week we were given our jump wings, Martin Luther King was shot and killed in Memphis. His death set off another round of violence in most of America's largest cities.

I had a long weekend between the end of my Airborne training and the beginning of Ranger School. I rented a car and drove to Fort Lauderdale to meet my father who had flown south on business. There were still a few hours of sunlight left when I pulled out of Columbus, Georgia, and headed for Fort Lauderdale. Driving through the star-filled night I listened to music and religious broadcasts on my AM radio and was comforted by the sight and smell of the red clay and pine trees that sped by my windows.

I arrived an hour before the sun rose over the motel where my father was staying. He would be awake soon, and I was trying to hold on to my resolve to talk with him about his war and the one I was training to fight. On the way down I decided to push past my father's defenses and my fear to tell him that I was worried I would not perform well in combat. Although I acted the part of the tough-guy SEAL, I knew this mask would not get me through the ordeal of Vietnam.

I checked into the motel, changed clothes, and went for a run on the beach. I watched the sunrise on the Atlantic turn the dark sky to pink and blue. When I got back to my room I called my father. We met for breakfast and the instant I saw him the courage I needed to talk to him in a different way disappeared. He asked me how things were going. I told him they were fine, just fine. I asked him how business was going, and his answer was the same as mine. He told me how proud he was of me and wanted to know how jump school had gone. When a business associate of his joined us, my father beamed as he told the man what I was doing.

In his book *Man's Search for Meaning,* the psychiatrist and Holocaust survivor Viktor Frankl made an observation that reminded me of this trip to Fort Lauderdale when I read it a few years ago. "Live as if you were living for the second time and had acted as wrongly the first time as you are about to act now," Dr. Frankl advised. I would like to have a chance to live that weekend a second time and have another chance to really talk with my father.

I drove back to Fort Benning on Sunday night. On the way I tried to understand why I was unable to have an intimate conversation with him. The most satisfactory answer was circular: because he is my dad and that is the way things are supposed to be. I should expect nothing else. Besides, the way things were looking, the war would be over long before I would have to go.

Army Ranger School was a tremendous confidence builder. I learned more about my limits and myself than I had in UDT or Airborne School combined. We spent three weeks at Benning, three weeks in the mountains around Dahlonega, Georgia, and three weeks in the swamps near Eglin Air Force Base on Florida's gulf coast. I learned to lead as many as four hundred men across unfamiliar terrain in unpredictable circumstances. I learned to plan with a life-or-death sense of urgency that overrode concerns about hunger, sleep, or weather. By the end of the course I was confident I could survive almost any condition on earth.

My orders gave me five days to get back to Coronado, and I decided to hitchhike across Alabama and Mississippi to Louisiana, spend a few days in New Orleans, and then fly to San Diego. On the road I saw poverty I had not imagined existed in America. The way so many people lived shocked me. Only the Lakota Sioux on the Pine Ridge Reservation endured conditions this bad. I stopped in towns and talked with white and black men about their lives. The black men were wary of my questioning and seemed relieved when I went on my way. The whites gave me their negative views of the federal government and Lyndon Johnson. In Mississippi I was picked up by a county sheriff who told me it was against the law to hitchhike. He drove me to his office and threatened to put me in jail. I sat across the desk from him while he played with his .38-caliber revolver. He smiled and said he would do me the favor of letting me go after a lecture about the need for outsiders to obey the law in the South.

Within days of my return to Coronado, Robert Kennedy was killed in Los Angeles. The image of him lying helpless on the floor of a hotel kitchen with his mouth open and his head in a growing pool of blood was all over the news. I grieved over Bobby Kennedy's death more than I had for his brother. I liked him because I thought he would end the war before it was time for me to go. My reasons were personal and not geopolitical. I had neither a deep-seated moral opposition to the war nor a reasoned alternative to fighting the Vietcong and the

North Vietnamese. I just preferred to miss this one if possible, and to do so without my having to refuse to go. As long as the war continued, it was my duty to serve, and I would serve enthusiastically.

I revealed my political confusion in a letter to my parents that summer. I told them I was glad Ronald Reagan had lost out in Miami but was sad that my choice, Nelson Rockefeller, had lost, too. I said I preferred the Democratic candidate, Eugene McCarthy, but would go with Nixon if Hubert Humphrey won the nomination. Nixon's secret plan to end the war was more appealing to me than Humphrey's vague promise to change things.

In the summer of 1968 I became administrative officer of SEAL Team One, a job most of us thought the worst imaginable because it was all paperwork. I also felt bad that many of the men I had trained with were already in Vietnam. Organizing an efficient flow of documents was not my idea of what a glamorous, swashbuckling SEAL officer should be doing. It was more like being president of a fraternity. To my parents I described the job as that of a child king. It was all responsibility with no real authority.

My job was to process the paper that documented the movements and lives of every man on the team and every piece of equipment assigned to us. Four enlisted men did most of the work, but I was responsible to the commanding officer if anything got lost or misplaced, and I took the assignment seriously.

While running this office, I learned that SEAL team deployments to Vietnam were unusual in two ways. Our orders were temporary duty (or TDY), which meant we stayed only six months. Platoons were operationally attached to the team's commanding officer in Coronado. Administratively, a platoon would be assigned to a navy command in Vietnam, but that command could not issue orders to conduct operations. They could offer suggestions, but the command to operate had to come from back in the States. I processed the reports that were filed after every combat operation, and as a result was often asked by our commanding officer to write recommendations for medals. Neither of these responsibilities made me more confident in the war effort.

The duty that eroded my confidence most was my visits to teammates who had been wounded in Vietnam. Most of them went to Balboa Naval Hospital, and I was surprised to see how changed they were. When I asked two of them who had been injured at the same time what had happened, they did not answer directly. Both had become deeply skeptical about the war and their contribution to winning it. Their attitude and the stories told by men I processed through my office lessened my disappointment at not being assigned to a platoon. The situation they described was beginning to sound hopeless. No one seemed optimistic that the war could be won, and few could give a compelling explanation of why we were continuing. Most advised me to do the best I could to get home alive. I still hoped that Nixon would win the election and implement his secret plan to end the war before I had to go.

Shortly after Labor Day I was assigned to a platoon to be led by Lieutenant Tim Wettack from Coffeyville, Kansas. Tim was also making his maiden tour to Vietnam. We were assigned twelve enlisted men, put in a rotation, and scheduled to leave in January 1969. Tim and I organized a series of training operations to get us as comfortable as possible working together. We practiced the three patrolling configurations used by SEAL platoons: all fourteen men led by the senior officer, seven men led either by one of the officers or one of the senior enlisted men, and two- or three-man groups. Our training emphasized the value of allowing men to make independent judgments without waiting for specific orders. To achieve this unity we needed time together.

We took our platoon to the SEAL camp near the Salton Sea and to the Chocolate Mountains. We went to Vallejo, California, a few miles north of San Francisco, to train with the PBRs, the navy's river patrol boats. And we spent a week at Eglin Air Force Base, operating as an aggressor force against the Army's Ranger trainees.

In Vallejo about a hundred army soldiers who were heading to Vietnam to join the Ninth Division were training with the riverboats. Their commanding officer challenged us to penetrate his nighttime perimeter. That night the clouds hid the stars, and under cover of darkness we not only penetrated their perimeter, we captured an army corporal asleep at his post. We bound his wrists behind his back and put duct tape over his mouth and eyes. We put an inflatable life preserver on him and swam him across a canal where we marched to our camp. On the way the only SEALs who spoke pretended to be speaking Vietnamese. We removed the tape from the corporal's mouth and in broken English ordered him to confess that he was a spy and to give us the name of his officer and the purpose of their mission. It did not take long before he told us everything. Then we made him get down on his knees and talk to his fellow soldiers over our radio. As he gave his name, rank, and serial number he broke down and cried. He wailed that he had held out as long as he could and begged the others to surrender so he could live. I felt terrible for him. We radioed his superior officer, gave him our approximate location, and said we would pop a red flare so he could find his missing soldier, who at this point was untied and kneeling on the ground. When we hit the flare the report sounded to our prisoner like a gunshot. He fell to the ground unconscious, thinking we had shot him. That night I learned how effective and de-structive terror could be, and I learned that the road to cruelty can be very easy to find.

At Eglin we went into the field for days at a time, searching out and ambushing Ranger patrols. One night we were cooking dinner in the woods and the smell of our food carried to the poorly fed soldiers. Three of them followed their noses to our camp and begged for some of our rations. Their faces were haunting. Their eyes were vacant, and they said they would do anything we asked if only we would feed them. These men were no longer in control of themselves. I hoped I never got that bad.

Early on election night it looked as though my hope for a Nixon victory might be disappointed after Humphrey won New York and Pennsylvania, and the numbers were close in Ohio and Illinois. But Nixon rallied and Nebraska gave the new president his biggest plurality. I voted for him because I took him at his word. Soon my hope for peace began to fade. In a letter home on November 26, I wrote:

> As expected the Johnson "peace talks" aren't
> progressing too well. From all indications it looks
> like they'll break the record for most days spent
> negotiating a settlement. We speculate quite a bit as
> to when the cease-fire will occur, and you have to
> give pretty good odds to find any money betting on
> a 1969 date. I occasionally find myself thinking that
> it would be better if nothing happens in Paris until
> we've made our deployment, so that we will not
> have wasted all of this time training.

My last leave began on December 20. Our whole family went on vacation to the Bahamas. I filled several sea bags with diving tanks, regulators, fins, masks, and snorkels so I could teach my brothers and sisters to dive. I invited a woman along whom I had dated off and on in high school and college. We had a great Christmas. I would never have another like it.

My father drove me to the Lincoln airport for the flight to San Diego. It was hot inside his four-door Buick in spite of a winter storm that had hit the town during the night. My dad started the car early to let the engine and heater run before we left the house. My mother said good-bye at the side door we always used for our comings and goings. As we backed out of the snowy driveway, I saw her standing in the kitchen window. Later my sister told me my mother cried when I was gone. She would have to cry twice. My flight was canceled, and I did not leave for good until the next day. Both days my father and I talked about everything but the war. The closest he got to saying he was worried was to tell me to be careful. I offered no easy way for him to broach the subject.

The Sunday before I left for Vietnam, Joe Namath led the New York Jets to a victory over Earl Morrall and the Baltimore Colts. No one had bet on that outcome, but we celebrated the victory anyway at the Down Winds, a favorite bar at the North Island Air Station. The evening ended in a fight between a group of pilots and us. One of them told us he would be flying with us to Vietnam.

Monday morning was hot and clear. We loaded our gear into a twin-engine prop plane that was slow but reliable. The noise of the engines filled my ears like wet cotton balls, and at first we could not hear each other speak.

Our seats were modified canvas slings, but the best ac-
commodations were on top of the six-foot wooden Con-ex
boxes that we used to transport our gear. Through the
sides of these containers I smelled the D-40 lubricant we
had sprayed on our weapons. It seemed as dark inside the
plane as it was light outside. I looked out one of the small
windows at the bright pink buildings and remembered
our boisterous farewell party the previous night.

I was pleased to be going over with Tim Wettack because I did not have to worry about his risking our lives
unnecessarily. Like me, he had no desire to be a hero.
Our definition of success was the same: do the job and
bring everyone home alive. At twenty-five, I was the third
or fourth oldest man in the group. A slight foreboding
welled up in my stomach. I had been late for the group
photograph because I had to stop at the flight center to
sign documents. Someone had joked that I was headed
for a bad ending because I would be missing from the picture. I told them I wasn't superstitious, but it did give me
one more thing to worry about. We would be in Vietnam
in twenty-four hours. Our training was over and I was
ready for my part in the war.

13

OUR DESTINATION WAS Cam Ranh Bay, a coastal city on the South China Sea, 120 miles northeast of Saigon. On approach in darkness we saw stars reflecting on the water, and white floodlight beams along the airstrip reached up to greet us. Behind these flickered dull, yellow lamps in the Vietnamese houses and shops. Farther back, the black and brooding land seemed annoyed by our arrival. It did not feel welcoming. Our plane rolled to a stop and the door opened. It was near midnight local time.

We climbed down to the longest concrete runway I had ever seen. Gary Parrott—senior officer of the platoon we were replacing—waited for us with a Vietnamese navy officer and frogman who would be our liaison with the

Army of the Republic of Vietnam (ARVN) and our interpreter. As we unloaded our gear into a pair of five-ton
trucks, the hot humid air carried the comforting fumes of
aromatic fuel mixed with an unfamiliar and wild scent. I
felt this was an outpost surrounded by life that did not
know or care about my training or purpose. We rode in
open trucks to the naval base on sandy roads leading
toward the ocean. I was on full alert to imaginary dan-
gers lurking in the shadows on either side of us. Ambush
seemed a real possibility. Wettack and I ordered our men
to stand at the ready with their rifles locked and loaded.
Parrott, smiling and relaxed, allowed us to make this
harmless mistake.

Gary Parrott seemed like a natural SEAL to me. I felt
toward him what Joe DiMaggio's teammates must have
felt when they first saw him play his rookie year. He was of
average height and weight and not at all imposing physically. If you did not know him and were asked to guess his
line of work, accounting might spring to mind, until you
looked at his eyes or followed him around for a few days.
When I saw Parrott's blue eyes I understood why some
writers used the word *sharp* to describe this part of the
human body. Whether a gift of birth or a trait he developed fly-fishing and hunting as a young man in Michigan, he could see things others missed. He was a man
who looked and listened more than he talked.

He fell in love with the people of Vietnam and their
land because it was still relatively undeveloped even after

thirty years of war. Gary had the gene that made explorers willing to risk it all to go where no man had been before. He preferred the outdoors and knew how to travel light. He was a great storyteller and one of the most sociable men I ever knew, but he seemed to prefer his own company.

He once told me how he loved bow-hunting deer because of the long wait for a quarry. Sitting in a tree from predawn to darkness without getting a single shot was not cause for complaint. To Gary it made the entire effort worthwhile. As a boy he had learned fly-fishing with James Jesus Angleton, who became famous searching for moles in the CIA. To understand how good Parrott's company could be, Angleton willed his beloved fly rod to him when he died. And to understand how far Gary would go to be alone, know that while he was a student at OCS he secretly lived in the abandoned and cavernous top floor of one of the school's administrative buildings.

Gary had scoped out Cam Ranh Bay before we arrived and told us what he had learned. It was a natural harbor that had been used by the Japanese during the Second World War. In 1965 the United States began converting it to one of our largest military installations. That it was also one of our safest made it a favorite stop for dignitaries, including President Johnson's in 1967.

As the navy's role in the war increased, the coastal patrol headquarters—code-named Market Time—was moved up from Saigon to the eastern side of the base, where there was a harbor and some world-class beaches. The navy installation included a communications station, a support facility, and joint service ammunition depot for coastal surveillance, river patrol, mobile riverine forces, as well as the Seventh Fleet's gunfire support destroyers and landing ships. A naval air facility was home base for the coastal surveillance aircraft.

Market Time's task, to patrol the entire coast of Vietnam, was a colossal undertaking. The distance from the demilitarized zone in the north to the Ca Mau Peninsula in the south was fifteen hundred miles. Market Time—or Task Force 115 as it was also known—was a joint navy and coast guard mission. The navy used a boat called a PCF (patrol craft fast) or swift boat along with coastal minesweepers. The Coast Guard used a WPB (a cutter). Farther out, the navy and the coast guard had high-speed gunboats, radar picket escort ships, and oceangoing minesweepers.

The swift boat, our platoon's principal means of transportation, was a fifty-foot-long, thirteen-foot-wide, quarter-inch aluminum alloy craft powered by two 480-horsepower GM diesel engines. With a maximum speed of thirty-two knots, the boat could make a 180-degree turn in seventy-five yards at twenty knots. Twin .50-caliber Browning machine guns were positioned at the boat's centerline in a gun tub mounted on top of the pilothouse. On the fantail was an eighty-one-millimeter trigger-fired mortar with a .50-caliber semiautomatic Browning fixed on top. The crew's weapons included M-60 machine guns, M-79 grenade launchers, M-16 rifles, 12-gauge shotguns, .38- and .45-caliber pistols, hand grenades, and occasionally C-4 explosives.

The swift boat was commissioned in 1965 when the war effort was ramped up to provide the navy with a boat for counterinsurgency warfare. They modified an all-metal crew boat used to service oil rigs in the Gulf of Mexico, and forty days later, the first two boats arrived in Vietnam.

The platoon we were replacing had not used the swift boats because they had been operating in the Mekong Delta, as were most inexperienced, first-tour platoons. They used PBRs or river patrol boats and were part of the Game Warden operation. They had accumulated six months' worth of intelligence on their area of operation, which was useless to us in Cam Ranh. Thus we were starting from scratch without the benefit of reliable intelligence and had essentially the entire coast of Vietnam as our area of operation. Since our mission was to set ambushes, abduct enemy personnel, and gather intelligence we hardly knew where to begin.

The day after we arrived at the naval base we reported to the offices of Captain Roy Hoffman, the commander of Task Force 115 which was composed of the swift boats and their support personnel. Hoffman was a tough, experienced officer who had volunteered for the navy during

World War II. He was discharged in the general downsizing that took place in 1948, and was recalled during the Korean conflict in 1950.

In Vietnam Captain Hoffman faced an enemy who did not have a navy. The enemy's coastal activity was mostly limited to moving small amounts of materiel and people. Our navy became so frustrated with the limited amount of combat that in late 1968 they combined the coastal command, Market Time, with the Mekong Delta command, Game Warden. The combined operation would be called Operation Sea Lord. This new command focused more and more attention on the rivers and canals of the Mekong Delta. As our efforts shifted, our tactics became more aggressive.

A December 1968 report filed by the commander of U.S. Naval Forces, Vietnam, to the commander in chief, U.S. Pacific Fleet, tells a lot about what was going on. During the entire month Market Time accounted for 49,264 "detections" and 20,656 "inspections." Destroyed were 669 junks or sampans and 736 structures; 1,119 "persons" were "detained," of whom 26 were "Vietcong suspects." There were 23 "hostile fire incidents" resulting in 68 "enemy casualties" by body count and 51 other "estimated casualties." Three U.S. Navy personnel were killed during the month.

In ordinary language this report says that swift boat crews physically inspected forty percent of the vessels they saw and destroyed about one out of thirty vessels they inspected, had one hostile fire incident for every one thousand inspections, and killed about three enemies per hostile fire incident. The ratio of enemy to U.S. dead was more than 20 to 1. For the Americans and South Vietnamese, each of those inspections, destroyed junks, sampans, and structures, and persons detained was a source of frustration. For the enemy each was a potential opportunity for recruitment.

Captain Hoffman briefed us on the success of Market Time and his plans to move farther up the Mekong River. He would provide us with swift boats for almost anything we wanted to do, but he had a limited number of helicopter gunships, and most of those were committed to covering the operations of his crews. He recommended we make contact with naval intelligence and with the army to gather a list of potential targets.

I left his office more confused than when I walked in. To say that I barely had a clue about what I would be doing in Vietnam understates the case. I was well trained in all the techniques of armed conflict, but I lacked a clear understanding of our enemy other than that they were opponents of our ally, the government of South Vietnam. No doubt Captain Hoffman was just as confused. As I said earlier, SEAL team platoons were not under the operational control of the commands they were assigned to in Vietnam. The commanding officer of SEAL Team One in Coronado retained operational authority over our patrol.

Everyone's experience in Vietnam was different, and it is impossible to generalize from my own. The war changed from year to year. Men who went to Vietnam in the early 1960s were participants in a war that was being conducted on a very small scale, mostly by South Vietnamese defending against North Vietnam's proxy, the National Liberation Front. By 1965 American soldiers and their South Vietnamese allies were fighting a large-scale classic conventional campaign against the North Vietnamese army. In 1969 the nature of the war was wildly different depending on where you were. In the central or northern provinces there were clearly defined battles between mostly American forces and the North Vietnamese. In the Mekong Delta, we were still more likely to face irregular forces with fewer weapons than we were organized North Vietnamese soldiers.

After 1969 the most important factor affecting a soldier's experience in Vietnam was the deterioration of troop morale. Drug use and racial tension became more common, and soldiers were more likely to believe that the South Vietnamese could not and would not win the war. Men who served in the Mekong Delta saw a different war than those in the central and northern provinces. The coastal areas were different from the interior. The major cities were more likely to seem peaceful than the countryside, though every place seemed peaceful just before fighting began. The last variable was the unit you served with. In 1969 an army soldier with the Ninth Division saw a different war than one with the First Air Cavalry. A marine with the First Division would not have recognized the war fought by navy SEALs. Pilots faced a different set of risks, as did navy Seabees or army engineers or for that matter any of the so-called support personnel who often found themselves at greater risk than a combat grunt.

After Wettack and I left Captain Hoffman's briefing, we faced the problem of deciding where to conduct our operations. Naval intelligence informed us that Vietcong soldiers carrying satchel charges—plastic explosives with small scrap metal pieces wrapped inside a canvas bag— had conducted an attack the night before we arrived. They hit a South Vietnamese perimeter near Phan Rang twenty miles to our south. One of the sappers was discovered crouching under a guard tower and shot, point blank, with an M-60. He had received medical attention because the South Vietnamese hoped to learn something from him.

They asked us to join in the interrogation, so Parrott, Wettack, and I drove down in a jeep. As we did, I realized how groundless my nighttime fears had been during our trip from the plane to our quarters. In daylight, the only obstacles to our safe passage were Americans moving in the other direction, headed for the beach carrying food, drink, chairs, and surfboards.

We found the Vietcong sapper in a field hospital; he lay dying on a canvas cot, wearing black silk shorts. Calluses covered his feet, and his short olive body was strong and lean. His thick black hair was cut short, and his eyes showed no fear. A liter bottle containing a solution of five percent dextrose hung from a pole, and a plastic tube carried the liquid through a needle into his veins. He wasn't receiving blood; his wounds had been cleaned and the bleeding stopped. The bullets had torn three holes in his chest and stomach.

He refused to answer any of our questions. Toward the end his eyes went blank, his mouth opened, and he labored mightily for breath. As I stood above him I tried to guess who he was. He was a few years older than I was. Perhaps he had joined the Vietcong after a family member had been killed. Unlike me he did not have a six-month tour of duty. His orders were to fight until the war ended or he was killed. His war was ending.

We learned from the ARVN officer who had interrogated him before we arrived that the dead man was one of six Vietcong who broke through the barbed-wire perimeter. All the rest had been killed, but not before they killed four South Vietnamese and wounded four. According to the ARVN officer, these men were part of a larger force operating in the mountains along the coast that was infrequently patrolled by ARVN soldiers. This area would be a perfect place for us to conduct patrols.

The next day we met with the army's Fifth Special Forces in Nha Trang twenty miles north of Cam Ranh. Nha Trang was a small port town with around one hundred thousand inhabitants. With a market for farmers and small businessmen of the central highlands, Nha Trang, like most major cities in Vietnam, became a center for U.S. military advisers, businessmen, and journalists. Although it lacked the glamour of Vung Tau or Saigon, it had one street with American bars, local prostitutes, and any other legal or illegal temptations.

The city had its share of enemy sympathizers and had suffered attacks from sappers who had killed civilians trying to get on with their lives. Getting on with your life was threatening behavior for both sides in this war. I was impressed by how normal civilian life managed to be despite the threats, violence, and perversions caused by the necessities of combat.

The Special Forces compound was a rectangle of nondescript army buildings. There we were told the coast offered little in the way of acceptable targets. Most of their work was conducted in the highlands, where we did not have authority to go. They identified some targets, including an island 130 miles to the north. Parrott suggested splitting the platoon in half. He would go north with Wettack and six enlisted men, and I would go south to the area where the sappers had hit the night we arrived in country.

Accompanying Wettack was the senior petty officer in our platoon and two of the most remarkable men I knew in the teams: Richard Solano and Richard Gore. Solano and Gore had become close friends in training; they were practically joined at the hip. When you thought of one you thought of the other. It was hard to say Solano without saying Gore. Both were fresh-faced young men in their early twenties, above-average athletes, and enthusiastic about everything they chose to do. They could turn a room full of men in foul moods into a bunch of dizzy optimists. Something about seeing these two made the day seem better, and we all preferred their company. Wettack had chosen well when he put them in his squad.

Mike Ambrose and Gerhard Klann, who had both done a previous tour to Vietnam, were my most experienced men. Gene Peterson was the quietest and probably our most reliable. Doc Schrier was our corpsman, and at thirty the oldest member of the platoon. Rick Knepper was our youngest and strongest. Bill Tucker was inarguably the best looking and the favorite of every female who encountered our group. A Vietnamese frogman was essential to our squad because he spoke the language and understood the people of Vietnam.

The coastal mountains south of Phan Rang were a natural hideout for Vietcong and their North Vietnamese army advisers. We did not know how large their forces were, but we had reason to believe they were large enough for us to be careful not to engage without the certainty that we could prevail. With my senior men's agreement I decided to set an ambush on a trail believed to be traveled by the enemy. This was my first operation, and I was excited by the prospect of finally getting some action. My plan called for us to leave our base an hour after sunset. A

swift boat would carry us to the beach below the mountains. The long slope of the beach would allow the boat to
stay outside of the surf line and still let us walk through
waist-deep water. We would patrol inland, set up the ambush, and spend the night awaiting traffic. If none came
we could leave our position an hour before sunrise, signal
the swift boat to pick us up, and return to base.

Our platoon had been on many training exercises
where we sat all night long in a mock ambush. Most of
what we did that night I had done before, but one element was new: sitting with a loaded M-16 across my
crossed legs knowing that I might have to give the order to
fire. My first kill-or-be-killed situation might occur soon. I
thought of the sapper and wondered if my rifle could do
that kind of damage. I knew it could and I knew the
enemy's AK-47s could do the same to me. The night was
uneventful. No one came down the trail. The only excitement occurred when the swift boat's captain made the
mistake of driving the boat through the surf to make our
extraction easier. He made it more difficult, and the boat
grounded on the beach. As the sun rose, seven well-
trained SEALs strained to turn the boat and push it back
out to sea.

14

M Y MEMORIES OF South Vietnam are almost entirely
of the Mekong Delta where the villages and small
towns and the many farms reminded me of Nebraska.
The headwaters of the Mekong are in the Tibetan Hi-
malayas, and the river drops over twenty thousand feet on
a journey of nearly three thousand miles across China,
Laos, Thailand, Cambodia, and Vietnam before its four
mouths fan out like giant arteries to form the richest natural river delta in the world. In that delta you can see the
fertile soil that creates wealth in the form of rice harvested
and sold at market. To produce as much food as the South
Vietnamese did without modern technology during wartime was an impressive accomplishment.

In the delta, away from the larger cities and American bases, the people tried to go about their business, raise their families, and survive the war. They tended to give their sympathy to whomever they feared the most. Either way they could lose. They risked having us destroy their villages if they cooperated with the Vietcong and having the Vietcong destroy their villages if they cooperated with us.

The war was corrupting everything. Journalists were willing to do anything to get a scoop, and businessmen and government officials were trying to make a buck. Military and political leaders struggled to look as good as possible, and alcohol, prostitution, and drugs prevailed. I knew no American who talked about winning the war or who seemed to believe we could. Though we were in a strong position militarily, it did not feel as if victory was right around the corner.

Much has been said and written about what the United States might have done to win in Vietnam. One view is that we simply had to apply more force to destroy the war-making abilities of North Vietnam. The proponents of this argument say: "We were fighting this war with one hand tied behind our backs. If you are going to fight a war, then you must be prepared to go all out to win it. In Vietnam, we simply weren't." According to this school, we proved this point when we drove Iraq out of Kuwait in 1991.

But this argument underestimates the determination of the North Vietnamese to pay the price necessary to win, unlike the Iraqis who surrendered to television crews. In Vietnam we applied considerable force in our effort to defeat the North Vietnamese and their ally, the National Liberation Front. In the end they defeated our B-52s with entrenching tools because we lost the battle for public opinion not only in the United States but also in South Vietnam's countryside.

I see three reasons for why we lost that battle. We became too closely allied with the former colonial power and, in too many minds, became just another western nation propping up a puppet regime in order to gain access to Vietnam's natural resources. "Throw the bums out!" is, as we know in our own political system, a very powerful battle cry. We did a terrible job of making it clear that the choice was freedom versus Communism. The word "freedom" not only had lost its appeal to people who just wanted the terror to end but also was discredited by our political and military tactics. Our military tactics on the ground—especially where I was in the delta—were appallingly counterproductive. In too many cases we applied too much force, not too little.

For Ho Chi Minh the cause was "freedom and independence." The words are chiseled into his mausoleum in Hanoi. As long as he lived, he was prepared to fight to the death for that cause. He and his compatriots demonstrated their willingness to go the distance with vision, bravery, and ruthlessness. To the North Vietnamese, "freedom and independence" meant freedom and independence from foreign control of Vietnam. In the south—which had the same battle cry—freedom and independence meant political freedom and independence from the north.

Freedom and independence were powerful words, especially when they had been sustained by Vietnamese freedom fighters for such a long time against such great odds. By the time the north chose to start the second Indochina war they had both tradition and great mythical heroes to rally the troops. They could even talk of the days when they fought alongside the Americans to free themselves from Japanese domination.

For the South Vietnamese and the American military who supported them, our "freedom and independence" campaign began as part of a greater global struggle for freedom, a cause that could hardly be expected to motivate farmers in the Mekong Delta. What did motivate many South Vietnamese was freedom for themselves and independence from northern domination. There were many more men and women in South Vietnam who were willing to die for the cause of freedom than public opinion in the United States cared to acknowledge.

South Vietnam's government was vulnerable to accusation of corruption because corruption is only visible in a government that is open and free. North Vietnam had plenty of corruption, but it was not visible to the press. In the modern world if you cannot put it on television, it does not exist. And there were plenty of stories about South Vietnamese corruption to put on television, stories

about coups and countercoups, religious minorities dem-
onstrating for more political rights, money that was being
siphoned off to accounts outside Vietnam, sex scandals,
involvement with the CIA, and military units that failed to
put up a good fight. All these and more were fair game in
South Vietnam. The fact that we neither read, heard, nor
saw stories about corruption in North Vietnam led us to
assume incorrectly that nothing of the kind was going on
there because their hearts were pure and good. There
were no protests in Hanoi because the government did
not allow freedom of expression, freedom of religion, or
freedom of assembly.

Making matters worse was this terrible truth: a free
and open government was a lot more vulnerable to the
subversive activities of the National Liberation Front,
which had the overthrow of South Vietnam's government
as its open objective. The government of South Vietnam
was in a lose-lose situation. If it responded with violence
and terror when the Vietcong used violence and terror to
establish control in the countryside, it would face public
criticism and likely increase the number of Vietnamese
who opposed the government; if it did nothing it lost
territory.

My simple view of the war is that it could not be won
because we focused too much on stopping Communism
and too little on building a free and independent nation.
We thought we could win a military war without winning
a political one and were bitterly wrong. We underestimated

the determination of our opponents, and we trivialized the willingness of our allies to pay the price necessary to succeed. For all these reasons, we had by 1969 lost our way and were merely looking for an honorable exit. We would discover there wasn't one.

Soldiers must learn to fight well and honorably without necessarily believing in the cause for which they put themselves into terrifying danger. Henry Abbott served with the Twentieth Regiment of Massachusetts Volunteers during the American Civil War and distinguished himself with brave and heroic conduct. He was killed standing up, directing his men during the Battle of the Wilderness in May 1864. Abbott was one of the pro-slavery Northerners known as Copperheads. He did not believe in the Northern cause and yet he volunteered, fought bravely, and was killed in the line of duty. This did not make him a mercenary. It made him an exemplary soldier.

Wettack and I tried to do our duty as we had been trained to do it. When Tim returned from Qui Nhon he reported that he had set up an unsuccessful ambush near a trail in bitter cold water and waited in vain for action. He and Gary Parrott thought it would be best if we found a position somewhere in the Mekong Delta rather than staying in Cam Ranh. After some discussion, we decided to split the platoon into two squads. My squad would go to Vung Tau to talk with the Market Time forces there and then confer with other SEAL platoons in the delta. But our main goal was to see whether we could find a stable area of operation. Tim would take his squad to the Ca Mau Peninsula where earlier SEAL platoons were located, since Parrott thought they would have access to much more reliable intelligence.

Vung Tau was another paradise location. It was on the tip of a half-moon bay that opened into the mouth of the Mekong River. The beaches were long and beautiful. Helicopter pilots and other American military came there for rest and relaxation, which meant the town was full of bars and prostitutes. We spent a few days talking to army and navy intelligence officers, American and Vietnamese, but could not find a suitable home for the entire platoon. We took a swift boat up to a barge near Vinh Long that supported the PBRs on the Co Chien River. We patrolled and set unsuccessful night ambushes for five days straight before moving to another barge at Ben Tre, where another SEAL platoon operated. I celebrated my first Buddhist New Year on the barge.

Then we went to Cat Lo, a town on the northern edge of Vung Tau Bay, and headquarters for one of the Market Time divisions. The officer in charge had not been informed of our arrival and was too busy with his own patrols to be very interested in ours. He agreed to provide us with boats for operations into an area of Thanh Phu province reportedly controlled by the Vietcong, but he was not willing to back us up with air or naval gunfire support.

Mike Ambrose, who had become my friend in UDT training and was my most trusted enlisted man, advised against going into the area. Mike was from Iowa and had made one tour immediately after Ranger School with an officer who was also a good friend of mine. Mike was quick and nimble on patrol and ran point on most of our operations. His experience made him valuable to me because I could trust him to make good independent judgments.

Mike was against our going into Thanh Phu because our Vietnamese scout was on leave. In the delta, an operation without an interpreter was more risky, and the lack of air support, though not unusual, was dangerous. Mike had also grown very negative about Vietnam. He thought we were wasting our energy because it was only a matter of time before we walked away from the war. This skepticism made survival his most important consideration when he gave me planning advice. So when we were told by the government of Vietnam's district chief that a high-level meeting would be taking place in a village called Thanh Phong in Thanh Phu province, Mike still thought we should pass on the operation. That the district chief said the entire village was Vietcong and that there would be no civilians present did nothing to change Mike's mind.

The district chief was an official of the South Vietnamese government and when he said there were no civilians in this village he made a statement that illustrates the tragedy of guerrilla wars. The government of South Vietnam was fighting against an enemy that included South as well as North Vietnamese. The tactics of the enemy against their own government included a range of activities from terror to simply passing on information about troop movements of the South Vietnamese and United States military forces.

So, when the district chief said the entire village was Vietcong, he meant that the men and women of this village had joined the forces of opposition to the government. The men and some of the women were probably part of the enemy's irregular forces that had lethal, though limited, capability. The chief knew there were innocent noncombatants in the village, but he warned us to take great care because the area was considered especially dangerous at night.

In the end I decided to do the operation. As an extra precaution I arranged to fly the terrain in daylight in a single-engine plane to identify the houses where the meeting would take place. That surveillance flight confirmed that there were no women and children in the area. I located the village on a map and then briefed the rest of the squad on the mission. Several hours after sundown we took a swift boat from Cat Lo up the canal to the village. The boat touched its bow on the shore and we scrambled on to the dry land. We waited in silence to make certain we had not been detected. Sweat ran in rivers down my back. Our plan was to move perpendicular to the canal for five hundred meters and then turn right another five hundred meters where we would find the meeting place.

Even without our Vietnamese scout the terrain was easy to navigate and we moved quickly. Along the canals the buffalo grass was high and lush providing dense cover for us and our enemy. Beyond this cover the land opened into rectangular rice fields, which lay fallow and dry. We walked along the top of the earthen dikes that surrounded the fields. Before the war villagers in places like Thanh Phong lived just above subsistence level by growing rice and fishing in the rivers and selling a little of their harvest in good years.

The people lived in thatch houses with bamboo walls and woven grass ceilings. The floors of these homes were usually covered with grass mats though sometimes even this luxury was outside their reach. During the war the people dug bunkers underneath the houses where they would go if there were attacks from the air. They used grass and smaller bamboo mats for mattresses and whatever fabric was available, often silk, to cover themselves at night. The entire family slept in a single bed.

The village and the area around it was described by the South Vietnamese government and by U.S. military as a Free Fire Zone. In essence this meant it was controlled by the enemy at night. In daylight, South Vietnamese forces might enter the area seeking intelligence about the movement of enemy forces, but they rarely went in at night. Thus, we expected to have the advantage of surprise on our side. It was about midnight when I told my point man to head out. The only noises we could hear were a few dogs barking in the distance. The night was quiet and calm.

My point man led the way. He came to a house he said he believed was occupied by sentries. We had been trained that in such situations it would be too risky to move forward knowing that they would warn the men in the village unless we killed them or aborted the mission. I did not have to give an order to begin the killing but I could have stopped it and I didn't.

In truth, I remember very little of what happened in a clear and reliable way. The pulse of my own blood was pounding in my ears. I no longer believed we had the element of surprise on our side, but I was still determined to proceed to the main village. At the village we approached the house where the meeting was to take place. Once again, we had been trained to approach a potentially hostile environment and the patrol required no orders from me. One man entered the building while six others remained outside to provide security from all angles of approach. We waited, spread out with one man on point, and from my position I did not see any security. Our point man came out of the house and whispered excitedly that the men were not there. No meeting was taking place and all the men were gone. He said their sleeping places had been recently abandoned. He went into two other houses and reported the same thing. When he came out of the second one he had a look of real fear on his face.

The women and children in each of the three houses woke, gathered outside, and began to talk loudly in high singsong voices. We knew we were in trouble. The absence of men told us we had been compromised. We were certain there were armed cadre in the village now on full alert. We had two choices: withdraw or continue to search houses in the dark. Before we could make the decision, someone shot at us from the direction of the women and children, trapping them in a cross fire. We returned a tremendous barrage of fire and began to withdraw, continuing to fire. I saw women and children in front of us being hit and cut to pieces. I heard their cries and other voices in the darkness as we made our retreat to the canal. We radioed the swift boat and moved quickly but carefully toward the canal. The possibility of being pursued or of being caught in an ambush ourselves seemed very real to me.

We came to the canal and hid in the buffalo grass in a semicircle facing outward for security. We heard the deep-throated boat engines approach and signaled our location with a small, red, handheld light. When the bow of the boat touched shore, we pulled ourselves on board. I could feel the screws turning in reverse and the boat swing out and away from land. In less than an hour, we were back at our base in Cat Lo.

I did not speak of my doubts on the way back to our base camp. Our actions were not considered out of the ordinary for guerrilla warfare where the number of civilian casualties is quite high. We cleaned our faces and our weapons before going to sleep for the few hours remaining in the night. At first light we packed our gear and drove to the port in Vung Tau, where we caught a ride on a destroyer that was heading north to Cam Ranh. Standing on the fantail of the destroyer watching the silvery wake recede behind us, I felt a sickness in my heart for what we had done.

The young, innocent man who went to Vietnam died that night. After that night, I no longer had illusions or objectivity about the war. I had become someone I did not recognize. I had been in Vietnam for five weeks and this was my first live firefight. It had not ended in the heroic way I had expected.

BACK AT CAM RANH I told myself that this war was not clean and that victory does not go to the warrior who languishes long in the backwaters of self-doubt and self-incrimination. We remained in Cam Ranh for a week waiting for Wettack to order us down to join him and the other squad. One night after dinner a messenger told me a radio transmission had been sent to me from the Fifth Special Forces in Nha Trang. It said a Vietcong sapper who had been working with a team of explosive specialists let his love of family get the better of him. He swam off an island near Nha Trang and turned himself in to the U.S. Army. He said he wanted to join a program called *chieu hoi*, which translates roughly into "open arms," meaning he would be allowed to go home if he gave us useful information. He became a *hoi chanh* and was not only willing to provide information, but volunteered to lead Americans to the other sappers on the island in exchange for his freedom.

The army colonel in command of the Special Forces told me it was a mission he would have loved to do but couldn't because he was shorthanded. If I could bring my men to Nha Trang immediately, he believed there would be time to conduct a successful operation. The sappers, operating on an island close to the harbor, had killed many civilians in Nha Trang. If we could kill or capture them, we would save a lot of lives.

I told Mike Ambrose about the message and ordered him to get the men ready for a possible mission. We boarded the swift boat and headed north. When we arrived in Nha Trang an army sergeant took us to the sapper. After a brief interrogation, I decided to do the operation. The plan was to go in quietly with the *hoi chanh* as our guide and capture the other sappers. Some of the senior officers argued unsuccessfully that we should not try to take prisoners; we should just kill them as they slept and leave.

With our *hoi chanh* we boarded the swift and headed east a mile beyond the island. The engines were idled long enough for us to drop two small rubber boats, which we paddled as quietly as possible to the seaward side of the island. It was one of the darkest nights we had in Vietnam making it ideal for this operation. I had every detail of what we would do in my mind. I was completely calm. We would land, hide our boats, hand climb a cliff to where our targets were sleeping, awaken them with force, bind and gag them with tape, and call for a helicopter to remove them to Nha Trang.

The landing and the climb up the cliff went well. We moved slowly through the rocky terrain. I kept the *hoi chanh* directly in front of me within arm's reach. He knew the terrain and quickly led us to his former comrades. The sappers were sleeping in two groups. We found the first group with no difficulty. I left four of my men close by them while I continued on to find the second. Once I reached them I would flash a small red light as a signal for the capture.

The second sleeping group was not where the defector told us they would be. He feared they were on the move. We saw them coming toward us. I dropped into a hurdler's position with my right leg extended in front of me. I had just fired a short burst when the crack of an explosion ripped the air. I was thrown backward and my rifle torn from my hands. I knew immediately I had been seriously wounded. I smelled burning flesh in the air. The pain was most intense in my right leg. In the darkness I reached my hands down toward my foot to assess the damage. The shape of it was gone. The foot was detached from the calf.

Gunfire rocked the night. We were under attack at close range. I had time only to tie a tourniquet around the leg above my knee. We were not yet out of trouble. Small-arms fire was coming in our direction. With difficulty I pulled myself upright so I could direct my men. They had begun to circle to get the enemy in cross fire. After they did the fighting did not last more than an hour. Then came silence. My corpsman had taken shrapnel in his eye and could not help me, but there wasn't much to be done. I broke a glass styrette of morphine and injected the drug into my thigh. Immediately I could taste it in my mouth. Gerhard Klann, our automatic weapons man, sat behind me and propped me up in his arms. He gave me an unfiltered Camel cigarette and I smoked while my radioman called for a medevac helicopter. All was quiet except for the city noise of Nha Trang.

The pilot would not land on the island. He lowered a sling and my men wrapped me inside it. As I rose from the rocks a finger on my left hand caught on a tree limb and broke. Thanks to the morphine I felt nothing. As the darkness of the island disappeared beneath me, the eastern sky began to show signs of morning; the ocean horizon was visible. Once I was in the chopper, medics cut my clothes away and added more morphine to my bloodstream. We landed, and before the chopper blades had gone silent, I heard the sounds of men running. I was car-

ried on a stretcher into a building I presumed was a hospital. As I faded into unconsciousness I had one thought:
my war was over.

I awoke in a hospital in Cam Ranh Bay. Ambrose and
two other men from the squad stood over me. They told
me I was being shipped back to the States through Japan.
We joked about how I had been injured because I missed
the group photo back in Coronado. We joked about how
messed up our tour had been. I told them I was sorry
things had not worked out as well as we had hoped, and I
wished them good luck with the new officer who would
be shipped over to replace me. The conversation was beginning to wear on us as I drifted in and out of consciousness. So we said our good-byes and parted company.

15

Two of the letters in my mother's collection were sent days after my injury. Both were written on American National Red Cross stationery. The first is dated March 15 and the second March 18. Neither is in my handwriting.

> Dear Folks:
> I suppose that by now you have received the singing
> telegram that your son was hit. I do not know
> exactly what condition or prognosis I am in but
> there is no immediate danger. I had a chunk blown
> away from my right foot. I will be having plastic
> surgery in Japan. I am in good spirits but part of my
> foot is in a bad way right now. After they work on

me for a while in Japan, I will be medevaced to a hospital near home. I would be writing this letter myself but my hands are bandaged. Later I shall write myself. Try not to worry as I am in good hands and I will be seeing you in a couple of weeks and am in good spirits. I do have a lot of exciting material for war stories and I will keep you all in stitches when I return. I will be able to walk again after they do some more surgery but now it really looks like hell, but will be OK.

The second reads

Dear Folks:

I made it to Yokosuka, Japan, Sunday night. They have a real good staff here and I'm being well taken care of. I have a lot of confidence in Dr. Bingham, the head orthopedic surgeon. He's going to take a look at my foot tomorrow morning. They'll probably send me from here to Great Lakes although I don't know when. I sort of have this Dr. Bingham labeled as the man I'd like to have operate on me, so I may spend more time here than ordinary.

I really hated to leave the platoon after having trained with them for so long. It's my only single regret about the incident. Perhaps I'm still dazed but I don't feel any bitterness about the war or anyone or any group of people. It looks like

everything is going to turn out all right. I'll write
again and keep you posted about my progress. Give
all my regards to the rest of the family. I'll be seeing
all of you shortly.

Both letters were full of lies. My injury was worse. I
didn't have any war stories worth telling. My fifty-plus
days in Vietnam seemed to me to be at best a waste of
time. I didn't hate to be leaving the platoon, and I was
happy to be going home even in the condition I was in. I
had convinced myself that my injury was retribution,
punishment, rather than a combat wound from heroic
duty. My spirit was in darkness. Like Jonah, the whale had
swallowed me; unlike him, I believed I would spend eter-
nity inside the belly of the beast.

I fell asleep in a nearly empty hospital ward on the
base in Cam Ranh. When I opened my eyes, I was in a
rectangular room with five other patients. It was night and
I guessed I must have slept through the entire flight.
There were six beds in the room and all were occupied.
Only one other patient was awake and he was making a
low, weak moaning sound full of sadness and pain. When
I turned my head to the right I could see him. He was
crying.

His left leg had been amputated above the knee. The
sheet was pulled back from the stump so that I looked directly into the bloody bandage wrapped around his
wound. While staring at him I fell asleep. When I woke

again the bandage was gone and I was looking at a cross section of his upper thigh. It looked like a piece of meat in a butcher shop. The femur had been neatly sawed, and to me it looked like the white eye of the Cyclops in a monster's face. I could not take my eyes off it, but once again I fell asleep. When I awoke, in the morning the man had been moved, his bed neatly made as though he had never been there at all.

In the clear light of day I saw I was in a single-story wood frame building that seemed more like a temporary clinic than a hospital. Looking out my window I saw a postcard-perfect green mountain in the distance. When my nurse appeared he confirmed that I was in Japan. He told me I would stay here for two or three days and then be shipped back to the States. He asked if I would like to call my family in Nebraska. I told him yes and later that morning he returned with a wheelchair. A five-foot-long piece of plywood extended from the seat and supported my right leg when he lifted me into the chair. He pushed me down the hallway to a phone. He dialed my parents' number. My father answered.

"Hello, Dad. It's me. I'm in Japan."

"Yes, we know. How are you?"

"I'm fine, just fine. The foot doesn't look too good, but there's a good chance they'll save it. Other than that I feel lucky to be alive. How is everyone there?"

"Fine. They are just fine. When are you coming home?"

"In a few days. I don't know which hospital yet. Maybe Denver or Chicago. I hope you can come."

"No problem. We'll be there. Do you know where you are now? I was in Yokohama in '46. Are you near Yokohama?"

"I don't know, Dad. I don't know where I am. Is Mom there?"

My mother and I had much the same conversation. I told her I was fine and that I would be home soon. I told her I loved her. She said she loved me, too. I said good-bye. She said good-bye. When the nurse lifted me back into bed I asked him about the man I had heard in the night. He told me he had died of a pulmonary embolism, a blood clot in the lungs. Early that afternoon I was loaded into a helicopter and taken to a larger hospital. There I was taken to an operating room. They told me they were going to do surgical debridement, which meant I would be injected with a general anesthetic, so they could scrub the wounds on my leg to reduce the chances of serious infection. I wasn't fully conscious again until the next morning. When I awoke I was in a room with only one other patient, a curious-looking man wearing a fluorescent purple robe and a shower cap. He was being treated for a scalp condition. He and I did not talk much.

When the doctor came around in the middle of the afternoon, he was not optimistic about saving any of the foot. "It's mostly blown away," he said. "So little is left it's not fair to call it a foot. But we leave the final cut to the surgeons in the States. Now we are only trying to remove as much of the debris as possible and keep the infections at bay. You'll have one more surgical debriding before you leave."

Then he asked me which hospital I would like to be sent to in the States. I asked what was available on the East Coast and chose Philadelphia because it was the farthest from home and the people I knew. I wanted to recover alone. I wanted as few visitors as possible. I did not want to have to answer questions about what I had done in the war.

After he left, I focused my attention on my damaged leg. I had no control over the nerves and muscles that seemed to writhe like snakes under the white plaster cast. One wave of contractions followed another, reminding me of my childhood coughing. Once the first cough came I could not stop the second, and soon an agonizing and exhausting crescendo of coughs ensued until my ears rang from the noise. I remembered the voice of my older brother, John, calling out to me in the dark garage from his bunk bed below, "Are you all right? Is everything OK?"

I missed that comforting voice and the childhood that seemed more permanently amputated from my life than my foot. I would certainly walk again, perhaps even run again. But I grieved more for my lost innocence, which could never be reattached to my spirit.

With my mind fully concentrated on my leg a miracle happened: the pain lifted. One instant the pain was with me; the next it was gone. It vanished. Disappeared. And in its place there was something that felt like much more than the absence of pain. What I felt was perfect clarity, perfect awareness. It was as if I had been blind and now could see.

I could see backward into my life with perfect recall of everything I had done beginning with my first conscious memory: I was two years old exploring a shed behind our house and hearing the frightened voice of my mother calling out to me. I saw how hard I had worked to do things that would please my parents and my friends. I saw how this had sometimes caused me to do things I should not have done. I saw and laughed at how foolishly I had behaved trying to be what I imagined others wanted me to be. A hero. A star. The strong one. The problem solver. The lifesaver.

I was free of pain and more peaceful and calm than I had ever been before or have been since. My life unfolded before my eyes like a motion picture run backward. I could see myself doing things I thought others would like and admire. I saw myself going along to get along, how I hid characteristics I believed were socially unacceptable. This willingness to conform and this need to be liked had become a habit so ingrained I had forgotten independent action was possible. The longer I acted out of concern for the opinions of others the more I became afraid of doing something that would displease them.

In the present I could also see things I would have

missed before. When I looked at inanimate objects, I saw into the depths of their beginnings. I saw the page of a book that once lived in a forest and the cowhide on a chair that was once a living animal. I saw the words of a magazine lying on a table and was certain I could hear the voices and know the lives of the writers of the stories inside. Even the man in the purple robe whom I had previously found uninteresting became a story worth hearing. He thought I needed help and buzzed the nurses. When they came to see what was the matter, I no longer saw people who were taking care of me; I saw men and women with lives, histories, problems, and value beyond satisfying my medical needs.

It was as if all time had been compressed into a single fraction of a moment, a kaleidoscope of possibilities I had not considered before. Somehow the whole of life had been opened to me. I saw that my own death was more than an inevitability to be feared but a necessary part of life to be embraced. I saw that the fear of losing something I valued—my property, popularity, my life—was what had enslaved me. Freedom would come when I could lose the fear of losing everything but my eternal soul. I laughed out loud from the happiness I felt at being able to see these things.

As the minutes wore on I became afraid that this new awareness would not last for long. The pain was going to return. This was going to become a memory I would want to remember. I needed to write down everything I saw and felt. Because my hands were bandaged, I tried without success to persuade someone, anyone, to record my thoughts. The more I worried about time running out the sooner came the moment when the pain began to return like a train far off in the distance. Closer and closer, louder and louder it became until I was back where I had been before.

The pain was with me again and I was left to wonder what had happened, wondering if there was any way for me to go back to that place where I had known such happiness, such peace, and such joy. Two days later I was on a plane with other wounded men being shipped to various places in the States. As the plane left Japan I watched the sun set over the islands. I saw the round distinct boundary of this ball of gas melt and flatten against the earth's horizon. It became a fiery, molten lake and then it disappeared. Daylight was gone and I slept.

When I awoke, the plane was still in darkness but we were motionless on the tarmac of a military base in Alaska having our plane refueled. The man who had been sleeping above me remained silent when I called him, and he was no longer dripping blood on my blanket. When the nurse came by I asked if he had died. She would not answer my question. "Get some rest," she said, and since she controlled the morphine dripping from the intravenous bag into my arm, she knew how to help me take her advice. I didn't know the man; he had been wounded and was flying home. Now he was gone.

When we landed at Fort Dix, New Jersey, I knew how Alice felt after she fell down the rabbit's hole. I had taken a drink from the bottle that made people smaller and had shrunk so I could get through the doors of this new life. Six young enlisted men in white uniforms carried us on stretchers to a gray U.S. Navy bus much like the one I rode from Providence to Newport a lifetime ago. The sun's brightness and warmth startled me. I squinted to see what was around me: more of the familiar military buildings with men coming and going, unloading the plane.

As soon as the driver had signed the form taking responsibility for us, we were on our way to the naval hospital in Philadelphia. My stretcher was suspended from slings attached to vertical chrome poles, which stood directly over the right rear wheels. Every pothole or bump in the road sent a shock wave up the poles through the slings to my body. The wave crested as it hit the white plaster cast on my right leg. As it did, my body would flinch in reflex. I cursed the driver, the road, and myself.

I was thankful when we finally pulled up to the semicircular entrance of the hospital, a circa-1930s building with two twelve-story towers and several long wings. We were lifted onto hospital gurneys, covered with cool sheets, and lined up for processing. A female nurse went from man to man, asking our names and checking our answers against the charts attached to us. A male attendant gave each of us a cardboard box. Inside we found a baloney sandwich on white bread, an apple, a hard-boiled egg, and a cookie. All four of my items went uneaten.

A dark-haired female nurse pushed my gurney down a long hallway with pale green walls and a brown linoleum floor toward an elevator. I watched the fluorescent light fixtures pass overhead. The elevator door opened and closed behind us. We were alone for one exciting moment until the elevator stopped and the door opened onto other floors, each time admitting another wounded man or two. All wore blue cotton robes over blue cotton pajamas. Some walked and some were pushed in wheelchairs.

As I observed the other patients, I remember thinking how remarkable it was that flying metal could produce such a wide variety of wounds on these male bodies without killing them. I was amazed at how a well-packed metal canister could destroy parts of a human being and still not end life. The mortars, box mines, howitzers, grenades, and bullets had exploded close enough to bring an untimely end to every man I passed that day. But they had lived on to face life in misshapen bodies. Their scar tissue would always tell a silent story to those initiated into the ways of damaged flesh.

Turning my head to the right I was startled to see a man in a wheelchair. He did not make a sound. He leaned toward me with the weight of his body resting on the elbow of his remaining arm. His right arm was missing above the elbow, as were both of his legs. I looked directly into his face except there was no face. In the place of eyes, nose, and lips was a sunken cavity smooth and free of scars. I thought of the boy in Dalton Trumbo's *Johnny Got His Gun* and wondered how he could have survived.

The English poet Wilford Owen survived some of the worst fighting of the First World War only to be killed a few days before the Armistice. He had seen how terrible flying steel can be and wrote about the moment it makes contact with the flesh of man:

> "O Jesus Christ! I'm hit," he said; and died
> Whether he vainly cursed, or prayed indeed,
> The Bullets chirped—In vain! Vain! Vain!
> Machine-guns chuckled—Tut-tut! Tut-tut!
> And the Big Gun guffawed.

But the man I was looking at had not died or at least his body had not. Somehow and for some reason he had lived. The door opened on the twelfth floor and I was rolled into quarters for sick and wounded navy and Marine Corps officers. This would be my new home.

16

MOST OF THE MEN ON THE twelfth floor were Marines
injured in the war. All of them were in the acute
stage of their treatment. The hospital must have been a
difficult organization to manage because you never knew
how many customers would be coming your way from
month to month. The pace of the war was the biggest variable, and I often wondered if there were ways to predict
how many amputees, paraplegics, and other wounded
would be produced when men go to war.

Most of the men had been injured very early in their
tours. This timing is quite common and is either the result of fateful coincidence, which is certainly possible in
war, or of frightful inexperience, which is a more likely
explanation. Gary Parrott and I once got into a discussion

about this fact and the unfairness of the medal system. I suggested a fairer way to give medals was to eliminate all but one, the Purple Heart, since this is the only one we can be certain the wounded deserve. Gary had a better idea. "Why not give a Purple Heart to everybody who goes into combat and then if they mess up and get injured, take it away from them."

At Philadelphia they took beds away from the patients instead. When I arrived, there was only one bed open on the floor and I was given it. They had taken it away from someone else. That's the way the place ran. Every bed was always in use so that every new arrival had to be preceded by a departure. Someone had to be discharged whenever a new man arrived. This simple physical law governed our hospital.

One way administrators accommodated the large number of customers was simply to add beds. This policy affected enlisted men more than it did officers. When we officers were well enough to go to the prosthetic clinic or when an event was scheduled on the hospital lawn, we had to pass by the enlisted men's wards. Not only were there ten or more beds in each room, but enlisted men also were expected to swab the decks and clean their own spaces.

We officers, on the other hand, lived in the lap of luxury. Two men shared a room and two rooms shared a bathroom. There was a solarium on the floor where we could gather to play cards, smoke, and watch television.

Orderlies kept everything clean and waxed. And we had a much better nurse-to-patient ratio.

I was assigned a bed in a room directly across from the nurse's station. The nurse who wheeled me in called for a male orderly to help lift me onto my bed. They asked if I needed anything, told me a doctor would be by shortly, and left. Turning my head to the right I met the eyes of my roommate, who had watched the entire unloading in silence.

His name was Jim Crotty and when he said his last name — with an elongated vowel that made me think of *crawdaddy* — I knew that Philadelphia was his home. He lay stiffly on top of his sheets, then pulled himself up with a trapeze that hung above him and said hello with a confident sincerity that made me like him immediately. He was not wearing a pajama top and his chest was covered with bright red eight-by-three-inch rectangles. His feet were bare and undamaged, but his ankles were wrapped in white gauze bandages that disappeared up his shortened pant legs and reappeared again above his waist stopping about midstomach.

The first question most men will ask when they meet another man who has been injured in the war is, What happened to you? Maybe this is a sign of a special bond between men who have suffered similar fates. Or maybe it isn't special at all and comes from the same robotic mindset that makes a passenger in a taxicab ask the driver, "Where are you from?" My wound was obviously caused by an explosion and required little explanation, but Jim Crotty's was not self-evident. He had been burned badly, that much was clear, but I had never seen burns cover so much of the body of a living person.

He had been training to become a Marine helicopter pilot when his chopper lost its tail rotor. He tried to land but when he came in hard, his fuel tank exploded. His crew chief was killed instantly, but he and his instructor managed to get free with minor injuries. Later as a nurse examined him, he watched large areas of the skin on his legs slough away as she tried to clean what he had thought were superficial wounds. He had third-degree burns that went from the tops of his shoes to just above his navel.

Third-degree burns destroy the skin. Only transplants can restore its vital protective function. The bright red rectangles on Jim's upper body were where skin had been cut, peeled away, and grafted to some part of his lower body. It was a long and painful process during which his grafts struggled with limited success to adapt to their new locations.

Circumferential burns pose a special problem because the patient always suffers the full weight of his body pressing down on the damaged and fragile surface no matter which way he lies. For a long time Jim had lived in a rotating contraption so the nurses could turn him easily and regularly. Recently he had been transferred to a normal bed. It had been months since he had stood upright, and it would be months more before his doctors would risk putting him in a vertical position because they were afraid it would result in the loss of some of the grafted areas.

As a result of lying down so long, Jim's body was flat and stiff as a board. For exercise he pulled himself up on his trapeze, which also kept him from getting bedsores and provided relief from the stress of being immobile. Once a day he was lifted onto a gurney and taken to another floor, where he was lowered into a whirlpool. Because his gauze bandages were stuck so tightly to dried blood, immersing him in water was the only way the nurses could change his dressings. The pain of this process caused him to thrash uncontrollably in the water, which darkened with his blood as though he were being attacked by piranhas.

Pain was Jim's constant companion. His doctor made certain he did not have to ask for relief. Dilaudid, the most powerful synthetic narcotic, was injected into his bloodstream every three hours around the clock. His regime was enlightened compared to the miserly way narcotics are typically administered to patients out of fear they will become addicts. Jim Crotty had most certainly become an addict who was physiologically dependent upon Dilaudid to control pain. However, he was not taking narcotics because he suffered from a need to substitute the temporary pleasure of the needle for the more difficult but longer lasting pleasures of life.

What surprised me was that even when he was under the influence of the narcotic, he was completely conscious. His speech was not slurred and his thoughts were expressed in clear and understandable sentences. If I had met him on the street, I could not have guessed that he was addicted to Dilaudid.

Jim came from Philadelphia and he taught me to eat scrapple, steak and onion sandwiches, and what seemed like a lifetime supply of Hostess Ho Hos and Ding Dongs brought by his mother and father. He taught me to write odes and poems to unique hospital objects like stump socks, those woolen garments worn over an amputee's limb in order to cushion the hard socket of the prosthesis. Jim had a lyrical gift and upon request would sing songs he had composed in a mock Joan Baez falsetto. I remember a couple of verses from his "Ode to a Stump Sock":

Wrapped in plastic clean and white
The stump sock waited in the night
On a shelf with all his friends;

He longed to have his eyes first sight
Of that special stump on which he might
Spend the life a stump sock spends.

Jim told me that we shared our bathroom with a man who was dying of brain cancer and another who had made his third unsuccessful suicide attempt. The cancer victim was already blind and bedridden, and his cries in the night would increase as his pain grew more intense and death came closer. The would-be suicide's name was Jackson Roark, a navy meteorologist from Boonville, Missouri. Jack was an alcoholic — a condition more common in the navy in 1969 than it is today — who became so depressed when he drank that on three occasions he had returned to his room and cut his throat. On the third try he came close to success. The loss of blood killed a large part of his brain, leaving him paralyzed on one side, unable to speak, and incapable of any but the most simple gestures.

Jim was not only up-to-date on the men in the next room, he knew everything happening on the floor and much of what was going on in the entire hospital because he didn't sleep at night. He lay awake blowing smoke rings and gossiping with nurses who were glad to have some company. He gathered stories like an attentive shopper.

He was in the middle of one of his stories when my doctor, a thirty-something orthopedic surgeon with coal black hair and a very noticeable limp, came into our room. He examined my medical records and the two blackened toes that protruded from the cast on my right leg.

"I'm afraid you have gangrene," he said. "I need to get you down to the casting room to see what's underneath." He said it would be painful and ordered an injection of Demerol, my favorite narcotic. I told him I would prefer to stay fully awake for this one, since he would probably be making the final decision about my foot. If he wanted to amputate, I wanted to have a say in the matter.

The casting room smelled of plaster dust and rubbing alcohol and had the look and feel of a high school industrial arts classroom. My doctor was talking with a man who held a power saw in his right hand. He hit the switch and brought the blade down toward my leg, and I was certain he was going to slip and cut through the cast to the flesh on the other side. But he cut only through the plaster from hip to toe, pried the cast apart with his hands, made another cut, and removed the entire casing like he was opening a lobster for dinner.

While the doctor pulled the dried bandages away, I had to be held down by a male nurse. With my leg exposed I saw the damage for the first time. In spite of the warnings of the doctors in Japan not to get my hopes up about saving the leg, I had done just that. One look at the mass of angry, swollen red tissue and my hopes crashed. It no longer resembled a leg. Bones stuck out at disorderly angles from flesh spread wide and flat across the blood-stained sheet. My ankle and heel were completely gone. The blackened toes were attached to my only remaining metacarpals, which were no longer attached to anything at all.

"We'll need to operate soon," the doctor said. "The infection is spreading. I'll come see you in your room."

Back in my room I asked for Demerol. As the nurse

prepared to stick a needle into my upper arm, I noted she was giving me a fifty-milligram dose and was thankful to the doctor for his generosity. The needle drove into my muscle and the taste of the drug entered my mouth. The pain didn't disappear; it seemed to move outside of my body where I could see it like a distant light. Crotty asked what was up, and I told him I thought I was headed for surgery because there was no chance of saving the leg. Minutes later the surgeon came by to tell me I was scheduled for the operating room in two hours. He asked if I was ready. "I'm up for it, Doc," I answered with false and groggy bravery.

Before the attendants from the operating room came to take me away I was visited by a group of patients in wheelchairs and on crutches. One of them, Jim Harwood, a swift boat commander whose left leg had been amputated below the knee, sat in a chair by Crotty's bed. He took his prosthesis off and got to the point quickly. He urged me clearly and passionately not to let them cut off any more than was absolutely necessary. "They'll play it safe in surgery. Don't let them do it. You'll need every inch you can get."

I thanked Harwood for his advice and closed my eyes to give it some thought. When I opened them the nurse was back with another needle, a preoperative tranquilizer and muscle relaxant. It was time to go.

17

I FADED IN AND OUT OF consciousness while I waited in the line of five or six gurneys outside the swinging doors of the operating room. When my turn came I was wheeled into the cold, bright space from which someone had just been wheeled out. Around me moved human figures covered in pale green surgical uniforms. Voices buzzed in my ears. I was lifted onto the table and an IV needle was inserted into a vein on the inside of my right arm near the elbow. My doctor placed his hand on my shoulder and asked how I was. "Fine," I replied, "just fine. And, Doc? You won't cut off more than you need, will you?" A mask went over my face and I was gone before he could answer.

When I opened my eyes I was in the recovery room. My mother and father were there, sitting in chairs against the wall. They were holding hands. My mother's eyes were red and puffy. "Mom? Dad? Is that you?" I called. They came to my bedside and looked down upon me. "How are you feeling?" my father asked me. "Fine," I answered. "Just fine." My mother held my hand and put a wet washcloth to my lips. Two other men were alone and still asleep in their beds. As my head cleared, I remembered where I was and what had just been done to me. I remembered my question to the surgeon, but could not lift my head high enough to see how much he had taken. "Do you need something, son?" my father asked. I addressed the answer to my mother. "Mom, I need to know how much is left. Tell me how much is left." She looked down at me, held my hand, and said, "There's a lot left, Bob. There is a lot left." She was not talking about my leg. From that moment I did not doubt that my body and spirit would heal.

My parents stayed a few days and when they left for Lincoln, I was relieved to be alone again. The hospital was a refuge I wanted for myself. I needed to separate myself from the past. Among my fellow patients I felt safe. I did not have to hide my deformities because we were all disfigured. We were a brotherhood of cripples, bound together by our deformities and by the indignities we endured. It is hard to remain self-centered seated on top of a stainless steel bedpan.

One day, when I was perched atop a pan, the woman

friend who had come to the Bahamas with my family and me walked into the room unannounced. She had been traveling abroad and had written me regularly from places like Cairo, Rome, and Athens. Her arrival at this moment embarrassed me and I asked her to leave. When I was finished with the bedpan and had called for the nurse, she came back into the room.

I couldn't bring myself to tell her how much I loved her for being brave and caring enough to come to my bedside. I said I was planning a trip back to Nebraska as soon as I could and hoped I could see her then. I told her I should be fitted with a prosthesis soon and would be able to run and swim and dance, and do all the things I had done prior to the injury. When she left, I was even more relieved than I had been with my mom and dad.

It takes a brave man to let someone they love see them as they are. It takes a brave man to allow himself to be loved. And it takes a brave man to ask for help. All three of these are blood relatives, and my reluctance about each was a child of the same fear. In time I would learn how big the payoff was from trusting the love of a woman who was not turned off by the way I looked. In time I would also learn that I should quit trying to go back to the way I had been. I would have to face the truth that there were things I could never do again in order that I might do things I never dreamed possible before.

In the beginning of my recovery, overcoming physical weakness was my most obsessive wish. One of the big moments on this road was the first day I was able to make my own way into the bathroom to urinate standing up. It is one of the great joys of male life. After lowering myself into the wheelchair and waiting for the dizziness to subside, I rolled to the doorway of the bathroom we shared with our neighbors, stood on one leg, and peed into the bowl. The only thing better would have been to be standing outdoors. The excitement of controlling my own stream was tempered somewhat by the sight of myself in the mirror. When I turned to wash my hands, I was surprised at how skinny and unhealthy I looked. I had already traveled a long way from the tanned and strong SEAL team look I had worked so hard to achieve.

All my training had produced a look I thought people admired. I had created an image for myself of being tough, self-reliant, physically strong, and imposing. Now, looking into the mirror, I saw a weak, pale, and scrawny man. This was not a face that would intimidate the bad guys and save the damsel in distress. It was the face of a man who would have to be saved by someone else. At first I neither recognized nor liked this scrawny, pathetic looking face. And I was reluctant to admit that I would have to ask others for help with even the simplest of tasks. Asking for help was not optional; it was essential in order to recover. What surprised me was learning that asking for help made me stronger than I had been before. But old habits die hard and for many years this new understanding did not govern me, though I was able to do something

I had not done very well before: feel sympathy for others. And I found that sympathy for others opened doors to a kind of learning I had not imagined was possible before.

I was drawn to the lives of new friends and to their stories. Lew Puller was the son of the most highly decorated officer in the history of the Marine Corps. Lew's wounds were terrible. On patrol with the First Marine Division near Hue City, he hit a trip wire stretched across the path by North Vietnamese soldiers. The wire pulled a fuse that detonated a 105-millimeter howitzer. The explosion threw him into the air and severed both legs just below his hips. His hands were mauled by the blast of metal, and his lower abdomen was pierced. The heat of the rapidly burning explosive cauterized his wounds and allowed just enough blood to remain in his system for him to live. The speedy arrival of a medevac helicopter saved him.

When Lew awoke, he learned what he had lost. The more conscious he became, the less he wanted to live. By the time he arrived at Philadelphia in October, he would neither eat nor make any effort to hold on to life. Not until his wife, Toddy, who was pregnant when he went overseas, brought his new son to see him, did Lew's desire to survive awaken. His boy gave him reason enough.

Shortly after I arrived, Lew's father came to see him. The stir his presence caused confused me. He was a general, but it was not his rank that impressed us. He was much more than just a general. This was Chesty Puller.

He had earned five Navy Crosses fighting in Haiti in the
1920s, in the banana wars in Nicaragua in the 1930s, in
the Pacific in the Second World War, and in Korea.
When I saw him, I understood how he got his nickname.
He was all chest. A short man with a face that launched a
thousand battles, his jaw was square, his lips full, and his
eyes sized up everything and everyone he saw. He asked
my name and the story of how I was injured. When I got
to the end of the firefight, his face drew so close to me I
could feel his hot breath when he asked: "Well? Did you
kill them? Did you kill them, son?" Here was a true warrior. Next to him I felt like an imposter.

Next to him we were all imposters. It was a heavy burden to be Chesty's son, especially if you were not physically equipped to follow in your father's footsteps. The son
had poor vision and lacked the athletic ability a combat
leader needed. He was taller than his father but much
thinner, and had the serious look of an intellectual. When
he graduated from college he was classified 4-F by his
draft board, unfit for military service. He persuaded the
board to reverse their decision and convinced the Marine
Corps to give him a try. He dedicated himself to becoming an infantry officer who would make his father proud.
When Lew shipped out to Vietnam he dreamt he would
someday sit on the porch of the family home in Saluda,
Virginia, drinking whiskey with his father and talking
about their wars.

Two years later I went home with him to Saluda. By

then he was in law school at William and Mary. His father had died a broken man from the pain of seeing his son so monstrously shattered. His mother was full of old school Southern charm with the steely will that enables one to survive tragedy through denial. She was dignified, aloof, and fully committed to the role of military wife. She served Lew, Toddy, and me iced tea. We sat on the porch and talked for an hour. It was not the conversation Lew had hoped to have.

In the hospital we listened and paid attention to each other. We were just wounded men with lots of stories to tell, and Crotty told us the best ones. He talked about the night a despondent patient climbed to the roof in hopeless and suicidal resignation because a nurse had not responded to his advances. He told us about the screams of our neighbor—who was dying of cancer—when his roommate crawled from his bed and with one pull removed his catheter.

The victim's roommate was Jack Roark, a challenging mystery. When his neurosurgeon told Crotty and me that so much of his brain was destroyed he would never be able to talk, we decided to try to reach him. Actually, we didn't reach him; a nurse did, and without even trying. She was blond and beautiful, with high Nordic cheekbones. She broke the heart of every man on the floor. Her body was stunning and her smooth pale skin turned my blood hot, but I could not gather courage to advance beyond mild flirtation.

One afternoon, while Roark was sitting in his wheel-chair by the nurses' workstation, my dream nurse came upon him as she went from room to room taking meal orders from the patients. The last person she asked was Roark. Believing there was no risk, she sat on the arms of his wheelchair, resting her magnificent thighs against him. She laughed and asked what he wanted for breakfast, lunch, and dinner. He responded, but not with words. When she heard the splashing sound and saw the yellow stains on her white stockings, she shrieked and retreated. In the small silence that followed, Roark pointed a bony finger at her and spoke his first words: "Lollipop. Nurse Lollipop." Roark had a poet's economy with words. Any man with such a gift could not be a hopeless case.

After he had been cleaned up we beckoned him into our room. Slowly he wheeled himself to the foot of our beds by pushing his good right foot against the floor. The scar from his surgery angled six inches up toward the top of his head. Roark had the thin, angular look of a man whose drinking had destroyed his stomach's capacity to absorb food. He had a heavy beard, which he infrequently shaved, and the hair on his head was beginning to grow back. His teeth were gapped and pointed. He looked like one of Faulkner's Snopeses.

Both Jim and I spoke to him but got no response. We asked questions he didn't answer. His eyes darted back and forth from one of us to the other. We could see he wanted to talk but could not form the words. Silence rose up in the spaces between the three of us. Failing in our first attempt at conversation, we resumed talking as though he was not in the room. Jim lit a cigarette and began to blow the elaborate smoke rings that he practiced all night long. The rings triggered a response from somewhere deep inside Jack's remaining gray matter. Holding up two fingers of his bony right hand and blowing the word out his nose like a horn, he said loud enough to be heard down the hall, "Cigarette!"

Jim gave him a cigarette and a light. Jack inhaled hungrily, burning a good half inch with his first drag. He exhaled and sat looking at Jim as a dog would look at his master at feeding time. So Jim gave him another cigarette. We resumed our questioning. What did you do before the hospital? Where were you stationed? Are you in the navy or the corps? Jack had a cigarette going in each hand.

When he was finished smoking he said, in a nasal voice that reminded me of Willie Nelson on helium, "Where and what and how as far as the weather business?" He spoke every word distinctly as if to savor the sound of each. Then he looked at us as though he had spoken for hours and had given us every detail of his life since his first childhood memory. Jack had confirmed his existence as a forecaster of weather and confirmed he knew his days of predicting rain were over.

Later on, after Jack had learned to propel himself by leaning forward and pushing the small front wheels of his chair, he composed a short phrase that perfectly summarized the condition of all the other patients on the floor. Six of us were playing cards and smoking in the solarium. Among the six we could count less than half the normal supply of arms and legs. Like some giant snail Jack rounded the corner, surveyed the scene, bummed a smoke, and sat contentedly, rocking his head side to side like one of those toy dogs you sometimes see in the rear window of a car. Then, holding up a bony finger, he proclaimed: "Absence! Artillery!" We stopped our talking and turned to him. I thought this man was a genius.

18

PART OF THE INTELLIGENCE of the human body is how quickly it forgets pain. It cannot be recalled no matter how hard you try or how much you pretend. It would be blasphemy to call healing, another characteristic of the human body, intelligence. Healing is miraculous. Certainly medical science and its practitioners contribute a lot to healing, but the body with no outside help does the most important work.

I have been witness to and beneficiary of this miracle. My wound was dirty. Metal, wood, dirt, and stone were driven deep into flesh and bone. The surgeons were reluctant to close the wound until they were certain the infection had abated. The disadvantage of this strategy was that it left a lot of scar tissue on the limb. The benefit was

I did not need to go back into surgery to have the wound reopened, which would shorten the limb. Among the amputees this was known as whittling you down. So I did not object to the stump being left wide open and cleaned by the nurses twice a day. Later, when infection was no longer a risk, a patch of skin from my right thigh would be peeled off and put over the end of the leg. If this graft took a prosthesis would be fitted.

During the early days and weeks after our amputations those of us with dirty wounds endured twice-a-day cleanings. None of us looked forward to these, and I have forgotten all but one. A nurse, standing at the end of my bed looking down at the stump of my right leg, began the first of the day's cleanings. I dreaded these because peeling the dried and sticking bandage was not just painful but gave me time to think about how painful it was going to be. It was the thinking that worked me into a sweat.

After all the dressings this nurse had changed and all the abuse she had taken in the process, she would have been within her rights as a normal woman to have become hardened to the repeated wailings of her patients. But she hadn't. We were not routine for her. In my case she tried to lessen my discomfort by beginning with the least difficult wound, directly on the tibia below the kneecap where there was an inch-deep gouge into which she had tucked a long strand of iodoform gauze. Finished with that she turned her attention to the end of my stump. Now the fun began.

She used hydrogen peroxide to remove the wrapping. Then she took cotton swabs and more peroxide to clean the bright red oval where my calf used to be. She used a heavy steel floor lamp to illuminate the shadows where I presume bacteria liked to hide. On this day as she began her work, she lifted the lamp by its neck to slide it a few inches closer to my bed. As she did this the base fell off and the shade end of the lamp came down violently on the exposed stump. The blow made me retreat against and up the wall. My nurse was horrified and apologetic and offered to request Demerol to make up for the accident. Because I knew the pain would subside quickly, I figured I had come out ahead on the exchange.

I was thoroughly enjoying my Demerol buzz when a man came into our room and introduced himself as a surgeon whose specialty was hands. From across the great canyon that stood between his nonsedated state of consciousness and mine, I heard him say, "I want to have a look at your right hand." He unwrapped the bandages and spoke again. "Can you open your fingers?"

"No," I told him, "I can't.

Since Japan the hand had been given little attention. I thought of it as belonging to someone else. It was clenched into a grotesque, tight fist. The bone on the heel of the hand, the fifth metacarpal, had been broken in several places. The bone was at least half an inch shorter now, and the pinky finger had turned at a right angle across the back of my hand. Both tendons on that finger had been cut making voluntary movement impossible. But the cut tendons were not the main problem. I couldn't open my hand because the joints were frozen in place from inactivity and from small metal fragments scattered through the flesh.

"We've got to get this working again," he told me, and with the hurried manner of a man with a long list of patients he left to order physical therapy for me. Weeks later he came back to examine the hand again. He was unhappy with my lack of progress. "Still can't extend the fingers?" he asked as he took my hand in his. Then, without warning, he took my index finger in his hands and with a pop snapped it open. Before I had time to protest he did the same with the middle and the ring fingers. "Now, keep them open," he said and left without a word.

On his next visit he was pleased with the results, but told me I would need surgery to fix the pinky finger and to slip one of the tendons from my ring finger over to the pinky. He scheduled the operation for the next Friday, the weekend I had been invited to dinner with some Philadelphia relatives of my father. So I asked for a local anesthetic because the recovery time would be shorter and because I wanted to stay awake to watch.

When Friday morning came I was wheeled downstairs to the hallway outside the operating rooms. I was surprised to see how many others were waiting on their gurneys for the next available table. I counted a train of ten other patients resting end to end. When my turn finally came, the anesthetist applied a block administered through a needle into my armpit. He asked me to tell him when I felt an electric current in each of my fingers. When I did he pushed in some juice. He repeated the process until all five were dead to the world.

It was as if the arm were no longer attached. No feeling remained and all control was gone. It was quite amazing. The surgeon began to scrub and prepare my left hand.

"Oh, Doc," I said, "I believe you have the wrong one."

"Really," he responded and rechecked the X ray in the light box. He turned the film over and proceeded. "Oops," he said. My least favorite word as a patient.

The surgeon began by rebreaking the hand with a hammer and a chisel. The arm bounced around like a frozen fish each time he struck it. Then he turned the pinky finger back and drilled pins into the bone to set it in place. He sutured up the hand and drilled a pin through the end of the pinky finger. After the cast was put on the arm he stretched a rubber band from this pin to a wire harness built into the cast. The tension kept the pinky from turning back to its earlier deformed position. Fifty years earlier a man with my injury would probably have lost the use of his hand. I was in high spirits when I returned to my room and ready to spend the weekend with my father's cousin.

Her name was Dr. Harriet Mitchell Arey. She was a pediatrician at Philadelphia Children's Hospital. Her mother was sister to Fannie, the woman who raised my father and his brother. Harriet was born in Duluth, Minnesota, in the home to which Fannie had sent John in 1928 after his year at Wentworth Military Academy. She was a little girl when John came, and she remembered him as handsome, funny, kind, and serious.

Harriet had heard about my injury from my father who had told Fannie's daughters, Jessie and Eva. When she invited me to her home, I was reluctant at first but ended up glad I went. In our short time together we became close enough to talk about the war. And the feeling of family in her home made me want to make a trip back to Nebraska.

I made arrangements for a three-day weekend in early June and got crutches rigged with a metal cradle on the right side on which I rested my cast. I flew to O'Hare in Chicago where I connected to Lincoln. As I hobbled the long distance between gates, I grew very tired, but what bothered me most were the stares at my empty pant leg. With each swing of my good foot, I imagined what people were thinking and seethed with rage at imaginary insults. My father picked me up at the Lincoln airport. We talked about my future plans on the drive home. The only thing I had in mind was a half-baked idea about attending business school and perhaps returning to pharmacy in some way.

The car windows were rolled down and the smell of early summer lilacs filled the air. When the car stopped in our driveway, I lurched through the breezeway into the house and thought of the many times I had run through this space with boundless energy. This time I was exhausted and collapsed wearily into a chair. I asked my mom to bring me a stool so I could elevate my leg to keep the stump from swelling. My dad took my suitcase down to my old bedroom. My two youngest sisters were still at home, and the five of us sat together uncomfortably and talked about their school and what was going on in town. Mom cooked a big welcome home dinner for the whole family, which gathered with much laughter around our dining table. She served wine—the first time my mother ever allowed alcoholic beverages at her table. The wine helped loosen our conversation, and for two hours we told stories from our past, laughed, and forgot what had brought us together.

That night I went to sleep in my old room downstairs. I was happy to be home, but when I tried to go to sleep I saw the people in Thanh Phong for the first time since I had come back. I heard their voices crying out to me. When I tried to put them out of my mind all I could see behind my closed eyes was a solid wall of blood. When I finally fell asleep my dreams were frightening. Something about being home had brought back these memories.

The following night the woman who had come to see me in Philadelphia invited me to her home for dinner with her family. I would not let their kindness penetrate the fortress of resistance I had built around me. When dinner was over, she drove me home. I wanted her to hold me and say that everything would be all right. Instead we kissed briefly, and I went back to my old room for a repeat performance of bad dreams and memories.

On Saturday night a friend picked me up and we drove to a bar in downtown Lincoln across from the Cornhusker Hotel, where friends from high school and college were drinking and shooting pool. I could not play pool but I could drink beer, and my friends made certain my glass was never empty. I needed help getting back to the car.

On Sunday I stayed home from church to avoid the questions, but I also no longer felt I belonged. Something had changed. The strong line that had been my connection to God had broken. Not even a thread connected me to the way I had been before. When the family got back from church we went to lunch, and both my mom and dad drove me to the airport. My father checked my bag through to Philadelphia. Both of them walked me to the gate. I was grateful for their love, but even more grateful to be leaving.

Soon after I returned I was fitted for my first prosthesis. The day I went to the clinic I was shocked by how difficult it was to adjust to it. The limb, made of wood, was larger and heavier than I had imagined and needed a cumbersome waist belt to hold it in place. I had dreamed of slipping it on and running and dancing. But I found I could not put my full weight on the leg without sharp pain, and could not wear it for more than an hour before swelling would make it difficult to take off and impossible to put back on.

The prosthetist in the clinic saw my disappointment. "Don't worry, son, it will get easier, a lot easier. You have got to learn early not to let this thing push you around." Every time I went to his clinic he offered the right mix of encouragement and advice. He wanted me to get well. He wanted me to do well.

Over the years I learned that for an amputee it is the prosthetist who is the most important, beginning with his advice to the surgeon about the size, shape, and other details of the limb. In my case I had extensive fragile scarring, which was broken down by the jarring friction of the prosthesis's hard socket. Broken skin does not heal well inside the dark, tight, hot, and moist environment of a prosthesis socket. Skin heals best in fresh, dry air, and with regular antiseptic cleanings. So sometimes I had to remove the leg for twenty-four to forty-eight hours and from time to time my prosthetist would advise me to have surgical revisions done to reduce the size of the remaining scar tissue. I had my last surgical revision nine years after I was discharged from Philadelphia.

In late May I left the hospital to go to the first annual Martin Luther King track meet at Villanova. I wanted to watch a Nebraskan, Charlie Green, run the hundred-yard dash. Bob Carlos, Charlie's competition for world's fastest human, was also entered. I went hoping to see a classic duel and it happened. Charlie won the race in near record time. After the race, I was taunted by a group of long-haired men who blocked the exit and knocked me to the ground as I pushed past them to leave. It was a reminder that life outside the hospital was more difficult than life inside.

Hospital life was protected and safe. Early in the summer John Zier, a Marine, asked me to go with him on his first trip home to Rye, New York, to visit his family. He had stepped on a box mine that tore one leg off above the knee and severely damaged the other. Now John was debating with his doctors about what to do with his other leg. His surgeon wanted to amputate it but John said no. He was determined to nurse it back to health.

John was a big man with wide shoulders and a naturally muscular body. He and his twin brother, Bobby, had gone to high school in Rye and earned football scholarships at George Washington University in Washington, D.C. They were starting offensive and defensive tackles for three years until they were kicked off the team for fighting. John met his wife, Linde, at GW. She was an art history major whose gentle ways were in sharp contrast to her husband. After the brothers graduated, they joined the Marine Corps, where their size and aggressive behavior were more prized.

John told stories of so many fights I began to categorize them. There were fights in bars, fights for revenge or the honor of his wife, fights begun by John and fights

started by Bobby, fights before he went to Vietnam and
fights while he was in country. There was even a small
category of fights he lost, but there was no category for
fights he didn't enjoy. Fighting was a hobby like golf.

He was a gifted storyteller with a high-pitched voice
that would squeak just a little when he got wound up in
some old memory. There was the fight at a party after a
fellow student took the unfortunate liberty of biting Linde
on her ass. There was another after Bobby had been
thrown out of a bar. He and John returned to the scene
and drove everyone behind a barricade of chairs they
built in self-defense. From behind this wall came a shower
of beer bottles, one of which hit Bobby and knocked him
out. That was the fight that got them kicked off the football team. There was the fight to avenge a friend who had
been beaten so badly he was hospitalized. John visited
him and kneeled close so the friend could whisper the
name of the bully in John's ear. Afterward, when the unsuspecting target opened his door, John hit him in the
face with the flat side of a trash can lid he had picked up
en route. And there was the fight with a man much
smaller than either Bobby or John who put each of them
on the floor with one blow to the head. "I think he must
have been a professional boxer. He had a great right
hand," John explained.

In Vietnam his fighting had a more useful purpose.
Once John was checking his perimeter and discovered

two men missing. Their breach of security put the entire company at risk, so John was understandably upset. The normal procedure would have been to court-martial them both. Instead John searched for them, found them watching a movie, warned them to prepare for a thrashing, and proceeded to do just that.

John Zier was neither a bully nor a braggart. He just wove his tales in from time to time as casually as he would an account of going to the grocery store for milk. He could tell about his mistakes as readily as his successes. Once John was leading a combat patrol that included some men who had just arrived in Vietnam. His compass man got them lost. In frustration John moved up the column so he was right behind the point man who was twenty or thirty meters in front. He saw the point man stop suddenly and motion with a closed fist to bring the column to a halt and drop down on the trail. John sent the same closed fist signal down the line and every man went down into firing position. John crawled up to talk with his point man.

"I saw figures, sir, moving across the trail up ahead about fifty meters."

"Where are they now?"

"Right after we stopped they hit the deck. I think they are still up there on the ground."

"What else did you see?"

His point man hesitated before answering. "They were carrying weapons, sir. I think they are Americans. I think they are ours."

Zier was livid at this news. He had cleared the area of operations. Only his company was meant to be out there. He whispered violently to the point man: "I'm going back to the radio to find out who the hell is out here where they're not supposed to be."

Again his point man hesitated. "Sir, I wouldn't do that. When I said they were ours, I meant our company. I think we've gone in a circle and cut off the rear of our column."

Zier's response impressed me more than all his fights. He laughed, signaled for his men to get up, and proceeded on. As he passed by the confused-looking Marines, he asked whom they were with.

"We're with some Lieutenant by the name of Zier."

"Oh," John hollered back. "I know him. He's a good man. You're in good hands."

On our trip to John's home Linde drove and I rode shotgun with John stretched out sideways in the backseat, telling stories full of drama and excitement. But when we reached the outskirts of Rye his mood changed and he became silent. At his house I saw the same scene I had played out in Lincoln. His mother and father came excitedly to the car. John needed to use a wheelchair to get into the house, and his dad helped him up the stairs. At dinner we talked but kept the subjects remote and light. On the mantel was a photograph of John and his brother. They were wearing their dress blue Marine uniforms. They had just become officers and looked as good as men could possibly look. Silently they gazed down upon us from inside their glass frame. They reminded us of what we used to be.

I loved retreating to the comfort of the hospital or to the houses of one of the married patients. I often visited Lew and Toddy's house on the naval base. Toddy cooked and kept us well supplied with beer. Lew and I and others drank and talked and listened to music. Lew loved Credence Clearwater Revival and had memorized the lyrics of "Fortunate Son." He would ask Toddy to cue the tape and turn up the volume. It became Lew's song.

By summer I learned the navy had recommended me for the congressional Medal of Honor for my actions on the night I was wounded. My men had recommended me for the Silver Star and it had been upgraded. The news stunned and embarrassed me. I did not believe the action deserved the highest honor.

In the fall I went back to San Diego to visit my friends in SEAL team. After my injury, another officer had replaced me and he had performed well. The platoon had returned from Vietnam with me as the only casualty. I loved these men, but we were now separated by our experiences. A gulf lay between us that we could not bridge. For us, subjects like loss and moral failure were taboo.

I did manage to talk to them of my reservations about accepting the Medal of Honor. Chief Petty Officer Barry Enoch, a man I respected for his fighting skill, told me I had no choice. "You must accept this award for everyone who should have been recognized but was not. You must wear it for others." On the flight back to Philadelphia I decided he was probably right. I did not like the idea of being known as a hero but disliked the idea of disappointing my teammates even more.

19

As soon as I was able to walk without crutches, I was ready to go home. The navy notified me I would be discharged and retired with a medical disability effective December 1, 1969. The hospital needed my bed a few days early, which was fine with me. I shipped all my belongings to Nebraska and planned on going home with only the clothes on my back.

Before leaving I called on Harriet Mitchell Arey to thank her for bringing me into her home and making me feel that I belonged. She told me I was welcome anytime and said I reminded her of my uncle John. "He didn't make it. I'm glad you did."

She was glad that I had come home alive. That's all she meant, no more and no less. I heard a lot more in her words. I heard her say I should make the most of this second chance; I should begin this second life with gratitude. I left Philadelphia determined to try.

Two memorable events happened the weekend I was released. The moratorium, the largest of the antiwar protests, took place in Washington, D.C., and Seymour Hersh's account of My Lai, where American soldiers massacred Vietnamese civilians, was published. I went home thinking my country was turning against me or I against it. Either way I wanted to escape. Hatred was in the air in the America of 1969. Though many sought to avoid it, the antiwar movement had become antimilitary. The hospital that had sheltered me was now releasing me. It was time to face the music.

My blue dress uniform fit poorly. A tailor in Newport, Rhode Island, had made it during Officer Candidate School. I had never worn it before and would never wear it again. It now hung loose on a body that had become considerably smaller during the previous eight months. I weighed less than 140 pounds, including my new wooden leg. A dark blue, wool peacoat hid my shrunken body but could not hide my puny face and scrawny neck.

I said farewell to the nurses on the floor and to my fellow patients, most of whom would be my friends all my life. An administrative officer escorted me down the elevators and the front steps where I met an off-duty nurse who had agreed to drive me to Fort Dix, New Jersey, where I could catch a ride on a military flight to Offutt

Air Force Base just south of Omaha. From there I would hitchhike the last fifty miles to Lincoln.

An icy wind found its way through the gap in my shirt collar and crawled down my back. I shivered and pulled the collar of my coat up around my ears. My new wooden leg was fastened to my right thigh with a leather strap. A wide scar across the shinbone of the stump of my right leg had broken open and bled as I walked. To lessen the pain from the scar tissue I shifted my weight to my left leg while I watched my breath spin like cotton candy in the wind and then disappear. I squeezed a rubber ball in my pocket to exercise my right hand to keep the fingers from becoming stiff and contracted.

Looking southwest across Packer Avenue I saw Veterans Stadium where Army and Navy would soon be playing their annual football game. A year ago I would have cared, but I had lost interest in the sport somewhere along the line. Farther south along Broad Street was the Navy Yard, where Lew and Toddy Puller were just beginning their day.

A bus drove up to the emergency entrance to my right. Corpsmen ran out with gurneys to unload the Marines from the bus. The left arm of one man fell limp and loose as they lifted him. He was in no condition for a box lunch. I wished them all well.

As I stood there bearing most of my weight on my left leg, I questioned my decision to take a military flight and then hitchhike home. A commercial flight with my father waiting to meet me would have been much easier. But I couldn't bear the thought of sitting with civilians or the idea of the long walk through O'Hare to change planes. And I wanted to be the master of this homecoming; I wanted to do this one alone.

I got lucky at Fort Dix and caught a space-available seat as soon as I got there. In two hours I was onboard heading west. The earth turned east below us, and I watched the sky change from blue to black. An air force officer on the plane offered to drive me as far as the interstate and said he would even be glad to take me all the way to Lincoln. I accepted the first half of his offer.

Standing in darkness on the shoulder of the highway I let a few cars and trucks pass before I stuck out my right thumb. The very first driver decided to stop after he had gone a good distance past me. My walk was more of a hop-step like Jingle Jones, the limping character played by Andy Devine in the television series *Wild Bill Hickok*. I almost yelled out, "Hey, Wild Bill, wait for me!"

There were four young men in the car, two in front and two in back. As I squeezed into the back my prosthesis began to pinch the skin behind my knee. I tried to shift my weight to ease the pain, but nothing worked. Gritting my teeth, I introduced myself. One of them told me they were students on their way home from the moratorium. The driver said he stopped because of my uniform. "We're not against the soldiers," he said, "just the war."

My views on the war had taken a U-turn while I was in

the hospital. The day I flipped from silent doubt to vocal opposition I was watching President Nixon on television. One line in his speech detonated a bomb inside me. "I've seen the ugly face of war. I know what you are going through," he said, and went on to give a rational explanation of the progress being made under Vietnamization, his plan to turn the war over to the Vietnamese. He appealed to America for unity. He got no support from me. "Bullshit," I said out loud. "You have no idea how ugly it is."

Bitter anger and resentment colored my view of all politicians and most political issues, especially the question of what to do in Vietnam. Men were dying and killing on both sides and in large numbers with little chance the outcome would be different as a consequence. Ending the war sooner rather than later seemed the only obvious and humane answer.

The students dropped me off in front of my parents' home. I thanked them for the lift and was grateful beyond words to be able to straighten my leg and end the pain of the prosthesis. As I walked the length of our driveway, my stump was swollen tight in its socket. The cold trickle of blood told me that my scar had broken down. My mother and father were standing in the doorway waiting for me. I ate a sandwich with them and told them I needed sleep. What I needed was to get my leg off and inspect the damage. In my small bedroom downstairs I dropped my trousers and removed the prosthesis. The sock covering the stump was bloody, and I felt great relief as I pulled it free of the hard socket. I took off my uniform, folding it neatly on a table, lay down on clean sheets, and went to sleep.

I was wakened at 2 A.M. by the same bloody nightmares I had during my last visit home. In the dream I saw the faces of the people I had killed and many more besides. They walked past me in an unending line. Their faces and bodies were mangled and rotting from their wounds. As they drew close every one of them asked the same question, "Why? Why did you do this to me?" I could not answer and I could not move. I was permanently mute and immobile. All I could do was listen to the cries and the identical, repeated question. Awake, I was too terrified to close my eyes again for fear I would fall asleep and the dream would return.

In the morning my father was eager to talk to me about my future. It was time to get to work on the plans I had made before I went into the navy. He had a friend who was willing to help me get into Stanford Business School in Palo Alto, California. I had doubts but did not speak of them while my mother served us a breakfast of eggs, bacon, toast, and juice. She sat down to join us. I looked into her eyes and tried to communicate what I was feeling. I believe she understood, but not a word passed between us.

My father's persistence and my lack of an alternative led me to apply to Stanford for the fall 1970 quarter. Meanwhile, I began looking for a pharmacy job and a place to live. I enrolled at the University of Nebraska to get used to studying again and signed up for a class in beginning accounting and one in political science on revolution. My brother Bill who was finishing college, agreed to share his apartment with me. I put away my navy uniforms and rejoined civilian life wishing to become anonymous.

The debate on the war was in full bloom. In Nebraska the opposition was centered at the university, and I attended several events where the speakers condemned both our involvement and President Nixon. At one, Don Walton, a reporter for the *Lincoln Star*, saw me and asked if he could call me to talk about the war. I said yes. During the interview he asked if I would go to Vietnam again knowing what I now knew. My answer was no, asking him in return if he would cross the street knowing he would get hit by a car. The headline of the morning paper read something like "Returning Veteran: I would not go again." Seeing the words made me wish I had kept my mouth shut.

Thanks to a man named Oliver Waite, I landed a job at Bryan Memorial Hospital, where I had been born. Dr. Waite managed the hospital's pharmacy and practiced dentistry in a private clinic. He had fought with the Marine Corps in two wars — against the Japanese in the Pacific and against the Communists in Korea — and he gave me the job because I had served. Perhaps for the same reason he hired two Cuban pharmacists driven from their homes by Castro.

Ollie knew what it was like to come home from a war and to feel bitterness toward your country. He told me how angry he had been when President Truman recalled men who had already served in World War II to fight in Korea rather than declaring war and using the draft. Ollie's experience with politicians had been far worse than mine, and the company of his remembered misery was comforting.

Standing for hours at a pharmacy counter was more difficult and painful than I had expected. I had to lean against a stool to make it through an eight-hour day and took so many aspirin that by the close of business my ears were ringing. Even without my physical problems, which I knew would heal in time, I had lost my enthusiasm for counting pills.

In my accounting class I met two women who helped me figure out where to go next. They invited me to their church and gave me the chance to join their circle of young friends. During their discussions of the Bible I brought in quotes from authors I was reading in political science: Hannah Arendt, Albert Camus, Bernard Fall, Jean Lacouture, and Tom Dooley. The women and the reading kindled a desire to pursue something other than business.

All through this time the nightmares continued, and I found no one I could trust enough to talk about them. The minister at Bethany Christian Church was a kind and considerate man who tried to help, but I would not let him in. When I went to church with the women from my accounting class, I began to feel close to something I needed: loving kindness and forgiveness. But I kept trying to substitute intellectual discussions of Camus and Arendt for healing. These served more as distractions than as serious self-examination. I simply did not know what to do.

I did know what to do about physical rehabilitation and began rebuilding my body with vigor and determination. Because my scar tissue continued to break down even under the stress of walking, running was out of the question. So I swam. Six days a week I went to the downtown YMCA and swam laps in a twenty-yard four-lane indoor pool. I did fifty laps up and back each morning. My leg was not waterproof, so I left it at the side of the pool. I wore a rubber band around the fingers of my right hand to hold them together. But once I was in the water I felt normal again. Slowly, surely, my strength returned.

Something else returned during the swimming hour. An hour in the silence of the water and the rhythm of the overhand crawl was like an hour of submerged meditation. I left the pool each day with an inner peace that stayed with me while I dressed, walked to a downtown restaurant, and had breakfast. I drank coffee and watched people hurrying to work. During these moments I started trying to understand what I had done in Vietnam and to consider what I should do now.

I had been assigned Camus's *The Rebel* in my political science class. It opens with a vividly authentic terrorist

assassination. Camus, who fought with the French underground, apparently had learned to use a knife. At least he
seemed to understand the techniques. Then I read another book by Camus entitled *The Fall*, which tells the
story of a man who was walking along the Seine in Paris
at night when he heard something fall into the water. It
could have been a body. He hesitated but did not stop,
convincing himself that the sound was something other
than a person in trouble. He tried to forget but the memory haunted him more and more. In the end he faced the
truth: he had allowed someone to drown because he did
not want to risk saving him.

At the beginning of the book I thought the title re-
ferred to the man who fell in the water. In the end it
was clear that the one who fell was the man who did not
save him. He believed he was a brave man, capable and
willing to risk his life for another. He believed he would
choose to do the right thing. But when the moment
came, he was a coward. The fall was his fall from grace.

The Fall reminded me of the doctrine of original sin,
which I had learned in church as a boy. According to this
teaching, we are all sinners at birth. Our fall—the legacy
of Adam and Eve's sins in the Garden of Eden—occurs at
birth. We are born into sin and can only be forgiven by accepting Christ. That is what I had been taught, and I had
believed it when my sins were still quite small. After the
war forgiveness did not seem as likely. My minister at
Bethany Christian Church told me I could be forgiven. He

said it didn't matter what I had done. He said God's capacity to forgive is absolute. All I had to do was ask and God would forgive me. So I asked. And waited for the change.

The change I wanted — to go back to the way I was as a child lying under the summer stars and dreaming, playing in a field near the red sandstone caves carved by the floodwaters of Dead Man's Creek, splayed out on the concrete by the pool at the country club where I caddied, oblivious to everything except the sight of a dark, cool wet mark where my face lay and the sounds of people splashing in the water — I could not make happen. I had suffered physical and spiritual loss, and I would just have to learn to live with it.

Second chances to correct mistakes are the stuff of movies, not life. I knew from the answer given to me in the Japanese hospital during the fifteen minutes I was in the eye of the storm that I had spent my life preparing for easy decisions and that when the difficult one came I wasn't ready. Physical stamina and intellectual strength were not enough.

Forgiveness came in small doses and at unexpected moments. I felt it during the movie *The Deer Hunter*. I was moved by the scene at a wedding when the bride and groom are sharing a ceremonial glass of red wine. According to tradition, if any wine spills it is an omen of bad luck to come. The camera draws close to the bride as her innocent mouth touches the wine. A drop falls from her lips and stains her white dress. No one sees it. She is unaware of the accident and betrays no sign of foreboding. Her new husband is sent to Vietnam and is horribly wounded. The lesson was the same: once the stain appears there is no turning back; there can be no second chance.

Grief at the loss of my innocence and the death of innocents followed me day and night. There were dark times when this grief would rise in my chest like hot water. I would become short of breath and feel that death was a better option than living. But I rejected that course of action. I could give meaning to the lives of the people I saw in my dreams only by choosing life. When the water of self-pity began to rise this was the rope I used to pull myself out.

During my physical recovery I had learned about the power of the only thing in life in which I completely believe: human kindness. Kindness—unselfish and unafraid—could lift my spirit most of all. My feelings of unworthiness dissolved the moment the new friends extended kindness to me. And better, worries about my loss ended when I learned that giving kindness was more liberating than receiving it.

Sister Prejean, a Catholic nun who ministers to death row inmates and to the families of their victims, once said, "Human beings are a lot more than the worst thing they have done in their lives." She spoke the truth. We are not as bad as our memories tell us we are.

In April a letter came from the navy informing me that President Nixon would present the congressional

Medal of Honor to me and twelve other men at the White House in May. I was still deeply skeptical of these honors and did not feel like a hero. I was still not sure I should accept and again considered refusing in protest. I was beginning to see the danger of believing that our greatest heroes live and die on battlefields. And I thought the medals were meant to make Americans feel better about the war.

When I was administrative officer of SEAL Team One, I dealt with the procedure for granting medals, and I knew that many men got nothing for bravery far greater than mine. There were five prerequisites for receiving a medal: Step one was the action itself. Step two was a living witness who had seen it. Step three was a living witness who could write (many a brave man's actions went unsung because the witness did not have a gift for words). Step four was a literate living witness who liked the brave man in question. No matter what the witness saw or how profound his gift for words, there would be no medal if he hated the brave man's guts. Step five was surviving the bureaucratic process. Even a brave man whom everyone liked could go without reward if his papers got lost in the bureaucratic shuffle.

All my doubts seemed small measured against the pride my parents felt. They wanted me to succeed and believed the award meant I had. For that reason, I decided to go to Washington and to bring all my brothers and sisters.

But the ceremony at the White House was scheduled

only days after the invasion of Cambodia and the killings at Kent State. My skepticism resurfaced as I wondered whether the award ceremony was an attempt to use us for political cover. On the plane heading east I talked to my father about my suspicion. I could tell he was worried I might do something rash.

We landed at National Airport in the early afternoon and were met by a naval attaché who escorted us to two black cars waiting to drive us to the Shoreham Hotel. None of us had been to the nation's capital before. The monuments and famous buildings dazzled me. This city was the place where history had been made, where the great debates had taken place, and great laws had been passed.

We checked into our hotel and were driven to the Mall to see the Lincoln Memorial and the Washington Monument. We explored the Capitol and got our picture taken on the Senate steps with Nebraska Senator Roman Hruska. We went to Arlington Cemetery and watched the ceremony at the Tomb of the Unknown Soldier. At day's end we saw the sun set on the Iwo Jima Memorial.

Our naval attaché took us to dinner at Trader Vic's. His quiet, respectful manner changed after he had downed three Suffering Bastards. Drunk, he was a loud and irritating bore. For two long hours he interrupted my mother and father when they tried to speak, complained about the navy, ordered the waiters to bring our food faster, and bragged about his underappreciated skills.

At the Shoreham I told my brother Bill to take revenge by pulling out all the stops on room service. Apparently I thought our escort officer was paying the bills. I said good night to my family and went to my room to inspect the day's damage to my leg and repair it as best that I could. The pounding had taken a toll on me physically, but not mentally. I was wide awake, so I went back downstairs to the bar and ordered a drink.

As I looked around the place, I wished I could share some of the pride my parents felt. I envied the moral clarity of their generation. I remembered the songs my parents listened to when I was a boy and imagined those tunes being played in the Shoreham thirty years earlier. I imagined the bar echoing with the music and the laughter of ghosts having a good time as they fought the good fight of the Second World War.

The next morning I awoke to discover that my stump had swollen so badly I almost could not put on my prosthesis. The fit was tight and painful. I took three aspirin and shoved a handful of tablets into the jacket of my tan navy uniform, which I would wear that day for the last time. Before I went downstairs I checked myself in the mirror and did not like the grim, unhappy face looking back at me. When I came off the elevator, everyone was waiting in the lobby — except my younger brother. He had taken up my challenge to order as much room service as possible and was working his way through a second tray when my father told him we were going to be late if he didn't finish.

We loaded into the two black cars and headed for the White House. Our route took us through Rock Creek Park and along the Potomac River. It was a glorious morning. The sky was clear and the sun bright, the air rich with the smell of flowers. We turned east and passed between the Lincoln Memorial and the Washington Monument. My heart was pounding with a pulse of dread and pride: dread of the ceremony, pride in my family. On the way, my father and I talked briefly. He was still worried I might do something foolish at the ceremony. He knew my dislike of medals and my distaste for President Nixon. The two might become an explosive mixture. He advised me to think about the future; my anger, he said, would subside in time.

A small group of sleepy-looking antiwar protestors were gathered on either side of the entrance as we drove through the White House gates. A Marine color guard stood at attention and saluted. The marble steps ahead looked insurmountable. I could not put my full weight on my right leg without producing a sharp pain. Each step increased the amount of sweat forming on my face, chest, and back. As I followed our naval attaché up the stairs to the second floor and turned right down the hallway, I smiled, thinking that perhaps my perspiration would produce a moment of genuine bonding with the often sweaty president.

The twelve families were arranged in a half circle facing an audience of the press, friends, military leaders, and a few members of Congress. A military band played. After a few bars of "Hail to the Chief," President Nixon came in and walked to a podium set up in front of us facing the audience, leaving him no choice but to turn his back on us.

The president's remarks were brief. We were heroes, he said, heroes in a heroic cause, the heroic cause of freedom. After he spoke, he moved around the half circle with a military aide beside him and placed the light blue ribbon and medal around each of our necks. My family was third or fourth in line. My mother wore a white short-sleeved dress with large gold buttons matching her metallic gold shoes. She wore a scarf around her neck and a corsage given to her by the navy. Her watch and wedding ring were her only jewelry. At fifty-six she looked young and happy, though her glasses gave her a serious look. Her bare hands, crossed in front of her, held the program that told the stories of the twelve men. The women of every family but ours were wearing gloves. My mother had insisted to my sisters that they would need gloves, but they convinced her they were unnecessary. She said she felt ashamed at this mistake, but it did not show in her face.

I let the president give me the medal. In truth I was badly confused. The war seemed like such a terrible mistake: politically, morally, and militarily. The suffering that was being inflicted on the people of Indochina did not seem worth the potential gain. Still I was moved by the ceremony and by the bravery of the other men who were there that day. There was something heroic about American men who were willing to travel to that strange country and fight for the freedom of people they did not know or understand. Nixon's words were not wrong. As much as I wanted the war to end quickly, and as strong as my belief that fighting on was futile, I could not deny how impressed I was by what these other men had done.

My dislike of President Nixon was more personal than political. I had believed him during the campaign of 1968 when he said he had a plan to end the war. I trusted him and it turned out he had lied. My trust betrayed I did not believe his plan for "peace with honor" would produce honor for any of the unfortunate Americans and Vietnamese who would fight on until an agreement could be reached. Perhaps there would be honor for the president or for Henry Kissinger, but not for very many others.

After the ceremony there was a reception for all of us, our families, and guests. The first thing I did was to take three more aspirin and drink a bottle of Coke. The president came by to shake all our hands again. I spoke with our hostess, Julie Nixon Eisenhower, and tried to be as charming as possible. She showed no interest in my charm. My ears were ringing and my body sweating from the aspirin. I wanted only to get back to the Shoreham to take off my leg. We were scheduled to fly out in the late afternoon and would be back in Lincoln that night. I had been in the nation's capital for a day and already I was eager to go home.

There was no parade in Lincoln to celebrate my

honor, which was just fine with me. I was pleased to be back in the shadow of anonymity. But the silence at other homes was not so easy for other young men who were changed by what they had seen and done, and needed the moral comfort of being welcomed and thanked by their communities. I had been to the White House, received the Medal of Honor, and enjoyed enough glory to salve some of my wounds. I measured the lack of response by the fact that the only letter I received was from a politician congratulating me on my award and thanking me for my service. His name was Jim Exon, and he had just won a primary election for governor. When politicians do not rush to have their pictures taken with Medal of Honor recipients, it is a sign that those who did not receive the medal were treated much worse.

Which is not to say I was treated badly. Just the opposite was true. My old friends, my family, and new friends welcomed me home. I was only harassed once at the track meet in Philadelphia. Other than that I was loved and cared for beyond anything I had a right to expect.

At work Ollie Waite and I spoke only a few words about the ceremony. I told him I was deeply moved by the Iwo Jima Memorial. He said he had never seen it. I told him I thought I did not deserve the medal. He said no one ever does. By then Stanford had accepted me, so I knew that when the semester ended my time at Bryan would as well. I thanked Ollie for giving me the job, but could not find words to do it adequately.

20

I CANNOT GIVE MEANING to remembering my life without remembering my father and his brother. From the moment of my father's death I began to think about the circumstances of his birth in a way I had not done before. Until then I had never thought of my father as an orphan. It had never occurred to me that he might have felt some responsibility for the death of his mother. I never asked what the Great War meant to his brother and to him. Indeed, I hardly thought about the Great War until my father asked me to find out what had happened to his brother. As I searched, I began to see a continuous thread from Versailles to the Philippines to Vietnam.

Just as the Cold War struggle between the Soviet Union

and the United States has been the defining political reality for my generation, I assumed the Depression and World War II were what defined my father's. As I look back at his life now it appears to me that the defining events of his life happened when he was a small boy. They were the Great War, the premature Armistice, and the failure of the diplomats in Versailles to establish the foundation for a lasting peace in the shambles of vanished empires. And just as I was completely unaware of the reality of the Cold War in 1948, the fifth year of my life, I know my father was unaware of the significance of the war, which ended in the fifth year of his.

Paul Fussell argues in *The Great War and Modern Memory* that World War I changed our way of thinking about the world around us. The Great War was a cataclysmic event that shattered the widely held view that humankind was making steady progress toward perfection. It divided modern European history in two. At President Lyndon Johnson's library in Austin, Texas, the curator once described the circumstances of Johnson's birth on August 27, 1908, in words that sum up how I feel about the Great War. "Times were so different when Johnson was born that it seems like those days were 'before' and we are living in 'after.'" It was the same for my uncle and my father. The Great War left a great no-man's-land between "then" and "now."

When my father and his brother were young, the men who were returning home from the war had experienced a trauma worse than any I had experienced in my life. Their entire generation had been laid on the altar for sacrifice. No one in my generation felt the way Wilfred Owen did when he wrote "The Parable of the Old Man and the Young":

> So Abram rose, and clave the wood, and went,
> And took the fire with him, and a knife.
> And as they sojourned both of them together,
> Isaac the first-born spake and said, My Father,
> Behold the preparations, fire and iron,
> But where the lamb for this burnt offering?
> Then Abram bound the youth with belts and straps,
> And builded parapets and trenches there,
> And stretched forth the knife to slay his son.
> When lo! An angel called him out of heaven,
> Saying, Lay not thy hand upon the lad,
> Neither do anything to him. Behold,
> A ram, caught in a thicket by its horns;
> Offer the Ram of Pride instead of him.
> But the old man would not so, but slew his son,
> And half the seed of Europe, one by one.

I doubt my father thought of this when he made his request of me. He just wanted me to know what happened on October 17, 1944, the day he believed his brother had died. I began to search for the answer in the summer of 1995 after my first term in the Senate and reelection to my second.

My search began at my youngest sister's farm where I could look through family records and letters she had gathered over the years. I was particularly interested in my mother's file of letters and her journal and in Vangie's letters to my parents. One letter described where John had been during the war and said that the Japanese had taken him prisoner. Another letter said that he had escaped and was alive. A third said he had disappeared again. And a fourth reported his death. There was a letter from General Douglas MacArthur that also said he had died.

Vangie's sister, Georgia, gave me a typewritten letter from John to Vangie, sent from the Philippines. The letter excited my imagination. It was erudite and witty, romantic and serious. It mentioned his family in Nebraska, which connected me to him. The date, November 17, did not indicate the year. Had it been written in 1941 before the Japanese attacked or afterward when John was operating with the guerrillas against the Japanese? The argument for a later date was that the envelope addressed Vangie as "Lt. Mella" and, in military style, did not have a postmark, suggesting it was mailed after the United States and Japan were at war.

An entire paragraph spoke of time they spent together at the Shoreham Hotel in Washington, D.C. He ended the letter with a plea to her: "Don't forget to remember, darling," and signed it "Wolf." Oh, how I loved that name. It suggested so much about John's nature and character. This was a man whose blood I was proud to share.

It was Georgia who told me that before he shipped out to the Philippines, John had driven alone with Vangie from Minneapolis to D.C., a fact that had scandalized her father. He became so angry he wouldn't speak to John, especially after Vangie secretly met him at the Shoreham Hotel.

I found two firsthand accounts of the guerrilla activity during the Japanese occupation of the Philippines. Both of the authors were still living but recalled very little about John. They did remember what happened to them from April 1942 until October 1944, when they served with a few hundred Americans allied with several thousand Filipinos in clandestine operations, spying on the Japanese and reporting what they learned to General MacArthur in Australia.

I read documents from the National Archives that contained the debriefings of the three men who were with John on October 17, 1944. Their account of the circumstances that led to John's death confirmed the one told to me by the American who commanded U.S. operations on that part of Luzon: John died because he made a single decision to follow his own instincts. Two years and ten months after the Japanese had attacked and invaded the Philippines, after he had fought in the defense of Bataan and had been surrendered, after he had survived by his wits as a guerrilla, he made one mistake and it cost him his life.

Vangie had not given up hope after Pearl Harbor. After John was surrendered on April 9, 1942, and disappeared, she joined the army and worked in army intelligence. She was certain he would survive. Late in the war Vangie worked in the Office of Strategic Services and then for the Central Intelligence Agency, which was created in 1947, where she remained until her death from cancer in 1975. She became a highly skilled and admired liaison with clandestine U.S. agents working in Eastern Europe against the Soviet Union.

On a night in the summer of 1995, I went to the Shoreham in order to imagine John and Vangie there in the spring of 1941. At the hotel, limousines and taxicabs were unloading guests for a banquet. The lobby was filled with conventioneers who had come to Washington to lobby Congress. I went to the bar, ordered a beer, and took it outside away from the sounds of laughter and the buzzing rumble of conversation. In the darkness I could hear cars racing along Rock Creek Park below. I sat by the pool where John and Vangie had swum. I closed my eyes and could hear John and Vangie talking and laughing in the pool.

I thought about John's last letter. He wrote it on October 4, 1944, to his aunt Sena, Fannie's daughter. He asked her to save ration stamps for apples because he expected to be home soon and would want some pie when he got there. He mentioned that he and four other men had arrived at headquarters. This particular event was later described to me in a letter from his commanding officer:

They came with some of our guerrillas from the area around the town of Tarlac. We were all in good spirits, anticipating the arrival of an American submarine. John seemed to be in excellent physical shape, too.

On October 14 John wrote a postscript to his letter: "What does everybody look like now? Can you send some pictures?"

Three days later on October 17 John and the four men left the command post for Baler Bay where they faced a fateful choice: a three-hour walk northwest through the mountains or a much shorter boat trip around the cape in an outrigger called a *banca*. They decided to go by boat, but when the motor sputtered out, everyone but John and one of the Filipinos began to walk. John managed to get the engine going again and they set off. But they never arrived at Dibut Bay, the rendezvous point with the sub.

John's commanding officer wrote me with the most likely explanation:

> For some reason they couldn't round the point and bring the banca into the bay. The winds were strong and the water outside the bay was pretty rough at the time. Whether they capsized or were being swept out to sea, I don't know. However, the Filipino was able to swim to shore but John did not make it. I talked to the Filipino after he came

ashore, but he was so upset and agitated that it was difficult to understand for sure what had happened. The others were taken out on the sub, and I'm sure gave statements concerning all their activities, including John's and the circumstances surrounding his death.

John had swum this same distance many times when he and my father spent summers with Fannie in Wisconsin. In a letter home to Vangie before the Japanese attack he said he was swimming regularly. Even in heavy seas it didn't seem likely he would give out halfway to shore. Suspicions were raised in the debriefing documents that John had been killed by the Japanese or by the Filipino who was with him. I do not know for certain what happened. However, this much is inarguable. John died on October 17, 1944. He would have lived if he had walked the trail with the other men and been taken to Australia. Three days after John's death, General MacArthur returned to the islands, as he had promised, to begin the second battle of the Philippines, the bloodiest clash of the war in the Pacific.

John almost made it home. He came within half a mile of being reunited with Vangie and his brother. He died because he made a bad decision. Somewhere in the murky sea beating the shores of the Philippines the water swallowed him. The story of my uncle came to an end.

21

I HAD A DREAM IN WHICH I met Uncle John. I awaken in a hotel room. The clock says three in the morning, and a ceiling fan turns slowly above me. The surf pounds on a distant beach. The light of a full moon transforms my white sheet into a pool of glistening mercury. My body looks dark against the bed's surface. I put on a pair of shorts and head for the beach. The moon lights everything within my view. I walk the sand, my senses at full alert. A premonition hangs in the air.

The air feels cool on my legs, chest, and back. My muscles are strong from exercise and rest. I am wearing my prosthesis but feel as if I could keep walking a great distance. Instead, I stop and turn to face the ocean. The place is Luzon and I am looking east into Baler Bay where my uncle drowned.

Rising steeply behind me are the remains of a volcano, its gray soil covered with lush vegetation. Fifty meters of sand separate the trees from the water's edge. I sit on the slope and feel as if I am in the bleachers watching a performance. My heels dig easily into the sand and I half squat in a resting position. Before me is the shimmering surface of the Philippine Sea.

Vietnam lies eight hundred miles west. The rhythm of the waves and the line of the moon's reflection create a mood of introspection and peace. Old memories are brought to life by the smell of the dark salty water. I remember moving through the surf with the inflatable rubber boats I used in the navy. I knew these waves could rise suddenly with the wind and understood how a storm could have ended my uncle's life.

The sound of the ocean, the smell of it, the taste of it, and the sight of it capture me completely. I am dizzy with the sensation of the night. In this reverie I do not see the swimmer in the water until he reaches the outer edge of the surf. He is coming directly toward me. He raises his head to see where he is going. I know from the many times I have swum into shore at night that he cannot see much beyond the general shape of the land. I can tell he is tired and weak. I think he may need help and move toward him. Premonition returns and my chest is gripped by fear. Fear becomes dread. I rise and move toward this man who now struggles to stand in the surging water.

We face each other on dry land. He is exhausted and disoriented by the water. Minutes elapse before he gets his bearings. Fear is in his eyes. As he sizes me up, fear changes quickly to anger. He is in his early thirties. He has the look of a natural athlete, about my height, but carries at least twenty more pounds. His hair is thinning and the square face and full lips make him handsome. I am impressed by how quickly he recovers from the ordeal of the swim.

He motions me to follow him up the beach and I do. We walk a path that rises up and away from the ocean before it turns to run parallel to the beach. We continue in silence for several miles. I ask him how much he knows about my life and his brother's. He does not answer. I ask him what happened to him after he escaped from the Japanese. No response. I tell him that I am sorry, and that I know he died because of a bad choice. When I tell him I have read his letters to Vangie, he turns to face me and a terrible sadness darkens his face. We continue until we reach a clearing that commands a view of the bay. At the edge of the clearing he finds a hiding place I would have missed. Inside there is a rough bench that I guess was used by men who watched enemy movements during the war. He motions to me to take a seat and he sits down beside me. No words pass between us. We sit and watch the bay.

I fall asleep and when I wake the moon is gone and so is my uncle. I am no longer on the beach; I am lying in the bed of my apartment, a mile from the Senate, my place of work. It is a half hour before sunrise, and I dress to go for a run to the Lincoln Memorial.

AUTHOR'S NOTE

ONE NIGHT OF MY LIFE as a combatant in the Vietnam War has been previously examined in great detail by the press and the public. I agreed to talk publicly about that night in part because I was trying to write about it for this book. I did not anticipate the intensity of the press interest and the public exposure that occurred to each of the six men I led that night. As a consequence, we gathered for the first time since the war to talk about our individual memories of what happened. The discussion that followed altered what I did and didn't remember. Thus, the story told in this book—though the most important details remain the same—is different than the one I first told, and even today I would not swear that my memory is 100% accurate. It is merely the best I can remember today.